Readers' Comments About the Book

"Michael seeks to memorialize the past in unforgettable ways… his book is a compelling tale of adventure which is almost impossible to put down." – Manus I. Midlarsky, *professor of political science and Moses and Annuta Back Professor of International Peace and Conflict Resolution, Rutgers University*

"It's very well-written and tells an extraordinary story with much passion, empathy and skill." – Omer Bartov, *professor of history and German studies and John P. Birkelund Distinguished Professor of European History, Brown University*

"…I would certainly draw students' attention to your book, as assigned reading in my course…" – Paul Hanebrink, *professor of history, Rutgers University*

"*Shards of War* reconstructs in vivid, sometimes heart-thumping, sometimes shattering, detail a central and remarkably unknown story of World War II, the improbable survival of a remnant of several hundred-thousand Polish Jews in the interior of the Soviet Union and in Central Asia. The intensely personal memoir, in part an adventure story, in part an exotic travelogue, always engaging and historically significant, tells of Michael's and his sister's odyssey from a home in Dubno, Ukraine, through a desperate flight ahead of the invading German armies, to the war-torn Soviet Union, into the Muslim towns and villages of Uzbekistan, and finally back to their home at war's end, only to discover the heartbreaking news that nearly all 8,000 Jews of their hometown had been shot and buried in mass graves. Michael's saga reflects the experience of so many survivors who have not told their story and offers a novel, unique perspective on events of World War II, absolutely essential to our understanding of the Holocaust." – Atina Grossmann, *professor of history, Faculty of Humanities and Social Sciences, Cooper Union, New York*

"This absorbing drama of teen siblings leaving their home and parents, fleeing the onslaught of the Germans on the Soviet Union, and surviving against insurmountable odds in Central Asia, portrays events of World War II and the Holocaust hardly covered in the literature. This unbelievable, yet true, unique story will serve well teachers to meet the New Jersey mandate that all students must learn about bias, prejudice and bigotry through the teaching of the Holocaust and genocide. The book provides an extraordinary example of the courageous, and often audacious, struggle of genocide victims to hold onto life and hope in the midst of unspeakable tragedy." – Dr. Paul B. Winkler, *Executive Director, New Jersey Commission on Holocaust Education*

To Rhoda, Nov 2010
the master editor, with
many thanks for all
your help.
From,

[signature]

SHARDS OF WAR—
FLEEING TO & FROM UZBEKISTAN

Michael G. Kesler, Ph.D.

Strategic Book Group
Durham, Connecticut

Strategic Book Group
P.O. Box 333
Durham, CT 06422
www.StrategicBookClub.com

ISBN: 978-1-60976-145-5

Printed in the United States of America

To Luba,
the hero of this story

In memory of my parents, grandmother, relatives, friends, and 8,000 compatriots in the mass graves on the outskirts of Dubno, Ukraine.

Table Of Contents

Foreword

I take great pleasure in writing this foreword to Michael Kesler's fascinating and significant memoir of survival in the face of impending annihilation. He tells a memorable tale that very few can tell, as the vast majority of Polish Jews did not survive the Holocaust. A youth sixteen years of age, and a sister three years older, flee their home in Ukraine ahead of the advancing German armies in June 1941. Suspense builds as the siblings escape east amidst roving German tanks and strafing aircraft. A few months later, the youngsters settle near Stalingrad where they spend a brutal winter, nearly perishing from hunger and cold. The following summer, they venture several thousand kilometers east, to Uzbekistan, where they survive, just barely, through the rest of the war, with the help of sympathetic Jews and non-Jews.

Being a native son of an American-born mother, I had no direct experience of the Holocaust. But attendance at a Yom Kippur Yizkor service (memorial service for the dead) in Israel many years ago had a lasting impact on me. This service happened to take place in one of the last transit camps for new immigrants arriving in Maabarot, Israel, after 1948. Most of the younger couples with children had already been placed in new housing, leaving only the older people who remembered all too well their losses. As the service proceeded, the extent of their agony became abundantly clear. I have never before, or since, heard such anguished weeping. It was as if the many dead, with the enormity of their suffering, had entered the consciousness of the living, and we were now hearing their cries of horror at experiencing their fate.

After the war, Michael and Luba return to their hometown and find it devastated, with nearly all its 8,000 Jews, including their family, in mass graves. Most of those who survived were those who, like Michael and Luba, had fled the German armies as they invaded Soviet territory, which included eastern Poland from 1939-1941. "Shards of War—Fleeing To & From Uzbekistan" chronicles the atrocities and mass executions of the Jews in Dubno and neighboring towns, as told by some of the survivors of these heinous crimes. When I think of the faces of the men at that Yizkor service long ago, I could easily see Michael as one of those survivors bitterly mourning the many dead of his family, friends, and townspeople.

Yet, as in many cases (sadly not all) of Holocaust survivors, the horrendous past is not necessarily a prologue to the future. At the end of the war, Michael and Luba depart for the West, ultimately arriving in the United States. The young people make highly successful lives here, including many children and grandchildren, and professional accomplishments at a very high level.

Surely, the tenacity of the human spirit is a legacy of their journey. But there is more. In writing this memoir, Michael seeks to memorialize the past in ways that will be unforgettable. Hence, we are not only exposed to the death and destruction of an entire European society, but also to a compelling tale of adventure. Once one starts reading this story, it is almost impossible to put down. Even though we know that the outcome is survival, the story is written in such a way that the suspense is carried from chapter to chapter. The reader is inexorably pulled forward. This was my experience in reading the book; I hope it will be the same for many more readers, especially younger ones who may identify with this tale of ultimate success in confrontation with overwhelming odds.

Manus I. Midlarsky

Moses and Annuta Back Professor of

International Peace and Conflict Resolution

Rutgers University, New Brunswick, N.J.

Author of *The Killing Trap: Genocide in the Twentieth Century*

Preface

Hitler's sudden, massive onslaught on June 22, 1941 caught the Soviet Union by surprise and proved disastrous to its armed forces. It also proved catastrophic for the Jews of the Soviet Union, sealing the fate of over one million Jews who lived in the western part of Ukraine. About 50,000 Jews, mostly young people, managed to flee the German armies advancing through Ukraine and spent the War years deep inside the Soviet Union. At War's end, finding their hometowns devastated and families and friends killed, most of the survivors became homeless refugees.

"Shards of War—Fleeing To & From Uzbekistan" relates the story of my sister and me fleeing our home in Dubno, in western Ukraine in 1941, ahead of the German armies, our stay in the Soviet Union, our return to Dubno — where all its 8,000 Jews had been murdered and buried in mass graves — and our migration to a displaced persons' camp in West Germany.

The book, written against the backdrop of the raging War, provides, in Appendix I, an overview of the Holocaust in Ukraine. Appendix II presents a brief account of the extermination of the Jews of my hometown. Appendix III gives a short description of Barbarossa, Hitler's code name for his war against the Soviet Union, focusing on the first, calamitous week of that war, and

1

Appendix IV presents a few selected maps.

In writing my memoir, I relived the events, thoughts, and feelings of the six most eventful years of my life. In the process, I have tried to reproduce faithfully, with my sister's help, many details of our experiences of 65-70 years ago. Unavoidably, I had to fictionalize some of the dialogue and names of people.

Prelude – Snapshots of My Life, 1932-1941

The Woods of Lublin, Poland – Summer of 1932

"Now, what is 17 x 17?" Father asked.

"Two-hundred eighty-nine," Luba, my sister, answered.

"And 16 x 17?" Father quizzed me.

"Two-seventy-two," I said.

Father loved to drill us on our hikes through the forest near Lublin, where he worked as a forester for the wealthy Polish landholder Graf Zamoyski. I still remember the sweet scent of the pinecones' sap glued to my fingers. I can feel the refreshing taste of the wild strawberries we picked as we reached a sun-soaked clearing in the woods. Our bags filled with hazelnuts and mushrooms and our faces stained with strawberry juice, we would return to our cottage triumphant to share our joy with Mother.

The villagers, most of whom worked for my father, treated us well, supplying all our needs from their nearby farms. They spoke to me gently, as if I were an adult, and made me feel important.

The teacher at the one-room school favored me and often called on me — at the age of seven being one of the youngest — to read aloud for the older kids, commenting, "That's the way to read!" I have often thought of those years as the sweetest in my life.

Fading Days in the Country – Fall of 1933

"Watch out!" a worker yelled at me one day as he saw me near a tree being felled by his co-workers. I ran to another part of the cleared area. I had sneaked out of school early to observe my father at work. Hundreds of workers filled the clearing as far as I could see, sawing the tall trees and using axes to slice away portions of the trunks. Other workers climbed on tall ladders and wrapped heavy ropes around strong branches of the tree on the opposite side of the sawing. Pulling on the ropes would bend the trees, making it easier to saw the trunks at the base and then fell them. I spotted my father dispatching workers and directing them in the various tasks with a commanding, quiet voice.

Father discovered me a few hours later and explained to me how each tree had to be trimmed, cut up, and prepared for various usages: home construction, shipbuilding, telephone poles, and so on, then moved by horse-and-wagon to many destinations. Father looked animated and joyful. I felt happy for him and proud to be his son.

One afternoon in late September, Mother opened a letter addressed to Father, stating that his services would no longer be needed. We soon learned that Graf Zamoyski had fired all Jews in his employ. Two weeks later, we left the forests of Lublin to return to our home in Dubno, a town of some 20,000 people—approximately half of them Jewish—some 200 kilometers to the east.

Awakening Tremors – Spring of 1935

The peaceful life in the forests of Lublin gave way to disturbing months of Father preparing, and then failing, to emigrate to Palestine, as the British had shut the gates for Jews to enter the Promised Land. Mother came to the rescue and opened a soft-goods store in Dubno's commercial district. Father at first hated becoming a small merchant, but soon adapted to the long hours of waiting for and serving customers, side-by-side with Mother.

The fourth-grade teachers of Polish literature and of history believed in a renewed period of enlightenment that had begun with the French Revolution and the birth of democracy in the United States. Further education, combined with technological progress, would bring "freedom, fraternity, and equality" to all mankind, they stated enthusiastically. The assigned readings of renowned, patriotic Polish writers Henryk Sienkiewicz and Adam Mickiewicz, as well as of Victor Hugo and Friedrich Schiller reinforced their rosy view of the future. And yet…

Luba had just been admitted to the gymnasium (high school); indeed, she had passed her entrance exams with ease. We soon learned that only a handful of Jewish students had been admitted for the fall semester. The town government had set up a quota that severely limited Jewish admittance to three percent, even though Jews constituted more than half the town's population.

"Will I be able to enter the gymnasium three years hence?" I wondered.

The Darkening Horizon – Spring of 1937

On the morning of Easter Sunday in April, Ukrainian church-goers poured out into Panienska, Dubno's main street, breaking into Jewish homes and stores, looting, and wounding a number of Jews.

A letter from my mother's sister in Warsaw brought new alarm to the family. An associate professor of history at Warsaw University, my Aunt Peshia had been dismissed and would soon come with her infant child, Heniek, to join my grandmother in town.

The afternoon hours at school filled me with worries of how to avoid attacks by gentile classmates on my way home with my Jewish friends, through the narrow streets and dilapidated passageways. A new, young history teacher replaced the elderly one. Tall, blond, and wearing a brown shirt, he extolled the virtues of fascism and of the great leader Hitler. One of the Jewish students snickered and caught the teacher's attention.

"What's your name?" the teacher asked.

"Yakov…," he stammered.

"Come here," the teacher demanded. He took hold of Yakov, tied up his hands with a small rope, forced him to crouch on the chair face down, pulled his pants down, and began to hit the boy with a cane. Yakov bled and screamed, while I cringed with fear and anger. I had never seen a teacher physically harm a pupil. The wild, angry look in the teacher's eyes, full of hatred, made me shiver.

"That's what we will do to all Jewish students who disrespect our great leader, Hitler," the teacher yelled. I ran home as soon as the class ended, and in the evening, told my parents of the incident. The next day, they transferred me to the Hebrew School and told me that in the fall they would enroll me at the Hebrew High School in Ostrog, about 60 kilometers east of Dubno.

The War Is Upon Us – June 1941

Hitler's armies broke through the Polish border on September 1, 1939, and moved swiftly eastward with tanks and heavy armor. A few days into the war, cars of evacuees from the west began to clog the cobblestone streets of Dubno. On September 12th, my parents decided to leave our home and stay with Ukrainian peasants, my father's friends, a few kilometers east of the town. We fled on foot at dusk, and next morning a Messerschmitt plane strafed the dirt road crowded with escaping refugees. Mother pulled me to roll into a ditch alongside the road. Screams of wounded people spread panic as we ran into the woods.

A few days later, the Soviet army moved westward, occupying the eastern half of Poland, including our hometown. We returned home and to our great surprise, found a strange Ukrainian family in our home. Father paid them off and they left, but the fear of losing our home filled me with worry. The Soviets ruled our town like a hoard of wild bears. They brought all commerce and business to a halt and carted off the goods. They treated everyone with equal contempt, and often, with brutality. And yet….

Father became employed again as a forester, working for the government. Luba, having completed the gymnasium, enrolled in the Rovno Teachers' Institute, some 30 kilometers north of our hometown. I felt relieved from taunts and rock-throwing by my classmates. We had become impoverished, but lost our fear of being singled out as Jews. I hoped the Soviets would not permit persecution of Jews within their borders. Life in our town moved on uneventfully, it seemed, and we began to adapt to an eerie normalcy, but for the ominous news from the West.

In the spring of 1940, Hitler's *Panzer* divisions broke through Holland and the Benelux countries into France. Six weeks later,

France capitulated, and the British army, some 80,000 men strong, barely escaped being wiped out by the German *Luftwaffe*. During the following 12 months, Hitler consolidated his grip on most of Europe while the Soviets became enmeshed in a disastrous war with Finland. In the spring of 1941, harbingers of Hitler's intentions to invade the Soviet Union darkened our horizon. Anxious talk between my parents and our neighbors of Hitler's violent persecution of Jews in Poland alarmed me. Early in June 1941, an air of despair descended on the Jews gripped by fear of an impending disaster.

CHAPTER 1

Leaving Home

The Day of Judgment

Split Decisions
I had just turned sixteen – I remember it well –
I was obsessed with the thought, nagging and sweet,
to surprise my classmate Sophie and tell
I admired her and would love her forever, indeed.
I saw Sophie once and never again...
On June 22, 1941,
the world I had known turned insane,
as Hitler's war on Russia had just begun.
On the third day of war, shocking news came
the Russians were fleeing and German tanks were near.
Then Stukkas roaring set the Castle aflame.
The day grew long, filled with panic and fear.
Yet the day was short, too short to abort
life planted firmly with patience,
sweat and blood of scores of generations.
Too short for the young to tear apart
from family, friends, and sweet ties of the heart.
Painful quarrels and bitter debate
erupted in each household, and led in dismay

to final verdicts of every Jew's fate:
who shall leave and who shall stay,
who shall live and who shall die....
As night descended, awesome and dark,
the gates of heaven shut, and Satan's verdict came stark:
all eight thousand would die, shot into pits,
except for a few who'd crawl out amidst
layers of bleeding, dying kin, into a jungle ruled by cruelty of chance,
hatred, violence and the Death-Angel's dance.

I have lived a long life, and I can readily tell my age from the way I find it ever more difficult to recall names of friends or many an event of yesteryear. So, how do I remember happenings and conversations of decades ago, you may ask. Some experiences have so profoundly changed me and my world, as to leave indelible scars on my mind. Memories of June 24, 1941, the day that I had left my home, have been haunting me all my life.

I remember the early morning sun peeking through the playful leaves of the acacia tree in front of my window, caressing my face as it awoke me on that fateful day. "Luba is here!" I dreamily whispered, hearing her voice in the adjoining room. I turned around and saw on the opposite wall the bedding on the open couch. It was true; she had returned. I felt relieved. Luba, my three-years-older sister, had been studying at the regional teachers' college in Rovno, a town some 30 kilometers northeast of our town, Dubno, in Ukraine.

Two days earlier, the Germans had invaded the Soviet Union, across the new 1939 border some 50 kilometers west of our hometown. My parents and I had worried if Luba would be cut off from us by war's turmoil.

I put on my trousers and shirt and ran into the common room, which comprised my parents' sleeping and dressing area, our dining facilities, and the heating stove. I glanced at Luba; I thought she looked beautiful. Her face had become more rounded, her lips fuller and broader, her grayish-green eyes larger and more animated, and her brown braid longer, reaching down to her waist. Now 19, she looked very much like Mother, short and slender with a narrow frame.

Luba sat across the table from Mother, flushed and excited. "Luba, it's great to see you," I said. "But, you look upset."

"Yes, the Germans have broken through the front, and the Soviets are fleeing," Luba said.

"How do you know that?" I asked.

She told me that her physics professor, a reserve colonel in the Red Army, had given her the bad news, asking her to go home and urge her family to leave Dubno immediately.

"Enough already! Stop your foolish talk!" Mother exclaimed. "You want me and Father to abandon our home and everything we worked for all our lives and run away like crazies?"

"We have a choice. We leave or we stay here and wait to be killed," Luba said.

"You think you and your professor know everything!" Mother shouted. "Napoleon tried to conquer Russia, and he didn't do so well. Let's hope Hitler does no better."

"In the meantime, his henchmen will probably kill us all!" Luba shouted back. Luba's boldness startled me. A few years earlier, I had been the favorite in the family, particularly of Mother. I also had been stronger than my rather fragile sister. Emboldened by my parents' love and my strength, I often acted as the superior sibling. What a difference the few years had made, I thought. Luba grew large in my eyes as I felt she was making much sense, challenging Mother.

Mother shot back, "We met the Austrians and some Germans during World War I and we lived on. It was the Ukrainians who killed my brother!" Mother screamed in a high-pitched voice, as she broke down and cried.

Mother often told us about her daring mission to ransom the severed head of her brother, Mehal, from Petlura's gang. My uncle, Mother's favorite sibling, whose name I bore, had been a lawyer and socialist leader in town, and among the first victims of the 1919 pogroms by the short-lived Ukrainian government under Simon Petlura.

Father returned from morning prayers at the *Shul* (Synagogue). He had come home the day before, on foot, to rejoin the family. He had been gone for weeks before, working 10-12 kilometers away as a forester for the Soviet government. He had been concerned by the outbreak of war, but reassuring news of the Soviet army beating back the Germans had uplifted his spirit. But now he looked like a changed man: his face, covered in perspiration and ashen, with froth at the corners of his lips, and eyes bloodshot and bulging as if ready to fall out, had a wild look about it. Father's demeanor, in sharp contrast to that of the quiet, even-tempered man I had known, frightened me.

"Moyne, you look terrible! What have you heard at the *Shul*? Mother asked.

"The Germans have broken through the front with lots of tanks. Some people think of leaving town," Father said.

"So what do you think, Moyne?"

"I think we should gather whatever belongings we can and leave before the Germans get here."

"What are we going to do? What are we going to live on? Leave everything and become homeless beggars in a foreign land? And what about Mother, my sister and brother?"

Uncle Mehal, after whom the author is named.

"Manya, all of us, particularly the children, are in mortal danger if we stay. I'm afraid Hitler is determined to kill all Jews," Father said.

"I know of Hitler's hatred of the Jews, but what good will it do for him to start mass-killing innocent civilians? How many Jews can Hitler kill? A thousand? Two thousand?" Mother answered.

The arguments, the shouting, the pleading went on and on. Mother went into the kitchen, and Luba joined her to prepare some food. I moved closer to Father and grabbed his hand; I wanted him to know that I agreed with him that we should leave.

"Momme is tough, isn't she?" he said with a forced smile.

"Don't be upset, Tatte. She'll change her mind yet," I said quietly. I felt for Father, understanding well his frustrations with Mother.

A talented woman, Mother was well-read and appeared more worldly than Father, who had come from a small village. Mother's father, a prominent lawyer, had died, leaving two sons and four daughters, Mother being the oldest. Barely 17, she and Grandmother began to manufacture candy and sell it at the candy store at the corner of the family's property. The havoc of World War I and the tragic loss of the oldest sibling, as well as a rather impoverished married life, had made her resilient and resourceful, but also quarrelsome and difficult; she exhibited an air of superiority towards Father.

Mother and Luba returned from the kitchen with poached eggs, fried potatoes, and salad, and we ate quietly. The heated arguments soon resumed, but it became clear that Mother's determination had prevailed and we would stay.

"I want to go and see Grandmother," I said, and I left. The street was flooded with sunlight, and the scent of acacia and lilacs filled the air. Fresh, lush greenery, set against a pale blue sky amid chirping birds, filled me with excitement. And yet, I felt choking in my throat as I thought of the quarrelsome exchanges at home. The panic in Father's eyes haunted me. I trusted him and his instincts, and the thought of leaving began to flood my mind.

I walked east on Berka Yoselevicza. I reached the end of our block. On the opposite corner of the side street stood the home of my Uncle Avrum, a large, white house with black shutters and a shingled roof. A pharmacist, quite prosperous, he had two daughters and a son who had left a few years earlier for Vilna.

I turned right onto a narrow side street. The din of rumbling vehicles surprised me as we approached Panienska, the main street of Dubno, where Grandma lived. Motorized vehicles and trucks filled with soldiers clogged the street. I turned left on Panienska and passed the Greek Orthodox Church, which Luba and I used to sneak into to listen to the beautiful choir during holiday services. The pogrom of 1937 had ended our curiosity and admiration.

I reached Grandma's home. In the front of the property stood the now abandoned, boarded-up candy store. The large, sprawling ranch house set back deeply in the yard, surrounded by tall oaks, contained Grandma's living quarters and a wing that she had rented out to a Soviet official.

My grandmother greeted me on the porch. A stout and healthy woman in her early 80s, she carried herself with dignity and aplomb, but a hard life left marks on her deeply wrinkled face. Her lips were folded, hardly visible, since she had few teeth left. I exchanged a few words with Grandmother, and then went to the backyard where Aunt Peshia and little Heniek were playing. I told my aunt of the arguments at home with Father and Luba wanting to leave and Mother insisting we stay.

"Your mother has seen a lot of tragedy in the past, and she

15

doesn't easily frighten, but I do fear the Germans," Aunt Peshia said. "I just listened to short-wave radio news from London of the Soviets retreating and suffering heavy losses."

"So, what are you and Heniek going to do?" I asked.

"I can't leave my mother alone, and I certainly can't take her with us; I have to stay. I think that you and Luba, at least, should leave, and the sooner the better," she said.

Her words and the tone of her voice startled me. I stood frozen, as she grabbed me.

"Give your aunt a hug," she said. "Be brave. Don't be afraid. Go!" she whispered. She then released me, and I left, deeply troubled: would I ever see her, Heniek, and Grandmother again?

The encounter with my aunt confirmed my feelings that we should leave, or at least Luba and I should leave if Mother persisted in staying. But I wanted to convince some of my friends to leave as well.

Sophie's name struck me like an electric shock. Sophie had been my classmate during the past two years and, in fact, took almost all the same courses I did. By far my smartest female classmate, often getting the highest scores, she became my tough competitor. The first year that I knew her, I treated her as a boy competing against me.

Last year I had begun to feel an attraction, a longing to be with her. She lived near the post office, halfway to our high school, only a kilometer from my home. I often would leave early in the morning and wait at the post office until I saw her at the corner. I would then dash out to greet her with the lame excuse of depositing a letter or delivering a package. A bit taller than I— everyone in class was taller—statuesque with light-brown hair and dark eyes, I thought her the most beautiful girl, and I hoped someday to marry her.

The author's grandmother, aunt, and cousin

Sophie lived with her mother and her maternal grandmother. Her father had passed away, and her mother, working in the hospital as a nurse, provided for the family.

I unlatched the door of the fenced yard of Sophie's home, and saw her at a table on the porch, reading a book. She looked up as she saw me approaching.

"What a surprise! What brings you here?"

"I thought I would stop by to say hello."

"And you haven't even had to take anything to the post office?" she said.

"Stop teasing me."

"I don't really want to tease you. I just want to let you know that you don't need an excuse to walk or talk with me. You know, we girls have a sixth sense; it's called intuition. I can tell very well that you like me, so you don't have to be so shy. You have nothing to fear, you know. Come, sit down."

She moved over to make room for me at the table. "Now, tell me why you really came."

I recounted to Sophie the heated discussions in my home and the dilemma of whether to stay or leave. I told her about my sister's message from her professor and about my brief meeting with my aunt, whom she knew well. I told her of my own feelings and urge to leave.

"Leave where?" she cried. "You know, tanks and airplanes can move much faster than one can by foot. If the Germans have broken through the Soviet Army's front, they will be able to conquer much of Ukraine in no time. And if they want to kill us, I'd much rather die here than somewhere in a strange place."

I listened. Then, mastering all my courage, I turned to her. "If Luba and I leave, will you come with us, will you come with me?" I heard my heart pound as I spoke those words and felt blood rush to my face.

"Mehal," she said, "you talk like a true teenager. You make it sound like a picnic, like a *lag b'omer* outing. Do you have an address to go to? I know that you like me and I like you too just a little bit, but I am not ready to run off with you, not at this troubling time."

She paused, got up, and put her hand on my shoulder. I got up to face her.

"Be serious, Mehal. My grandmother is ill, my mother works hard to support us, and we try so very hard to be together and survive. How could I possibly leave my mother alone?" Agitated and blushing, she spoke with gentleness that belied the firmness.

Suddenly, an explosion rocked the house and the yard. We looked up and saw several Stukkas dropping bomb—like inverted finned bottles—near the Castle along the Ikva River across from the high school. Powerful explosions came in succession.

"Oh my God! Oh my God!" Sophie screamed and fell into my arms, trembling with fear. She embraced me, and the warmth of her body overwhelmed me. Tremors ran through me and I became transported, as if in a dream. I gently caressed her face.

"Sophie! Sophie, darling! What's happening?" shouted her grandmother, coming down the stairs.

Sophie abruptly pushed me aside. "Mehal, you better leave. Run back to your home!" she said and ran inside to her grandmother.

Shocked as if somebody had torn a part of me, I felt hurt and angry. Sophie had dismissed me as if I did not matter. Then a dark, sorrowful thought overwhelmed me, that I might not see Sophie ever again! I felt abandoned, yet more determined to leave.

I ran home through Panienska, past the Great Synagogue on the hill, and turned onto Berka Yoselevicza. Frightened and agitated people filled the street in clusters, moving in excitement, as bees around a beehive. Startled by the dramatic change, I rushed down the street that only a few hours earlier had been so quiet.

I reached my home to find Luba in front of our house, buttonholing neighboring friends. As I approached, Luba turned sharply towards me. "Where have you been? Mother wants us to leave. German armored vehicles have been sighted in Mlynov, just a few kilometers from here."

"Why did she change her mind?"

"The Feyersteins from across the street came over and pleaded with her that she should let us go since the Germans would almost certainly grab the young men first, and Mother wanted me to go with you."

We entered the house, and I saw Mother packing two small valises with underwear, a change of clothes, and a couple of sweaters. She had also prepared a few sandwiches and found our leather winter boots.

"Father and I decided you and Luba should go, and we will stay here. The Germans will not bother us old people, but they may well take you, Mehal, away. So, we want you and Luba to leave, maybe for a day, maybe forever," she said as she broke down and cried.

I watched my mother turn into a defeated woman. It seemed as if all the awesome burdens of a difficult life converged to crush her. Her eyes turned dull, her lips tightened, and her cheeks turned pale; her wiry, erect frame stooped like a folded accordion gone silent.

Then, as if awakened, she said, "If you have to move farther east, head towards Aunt Etie in Ostrog. I'm sure she and Uncle Sholem will welcome you. You liked them, didn't you, Mehal, when you studied there?"

The day's painful, quarrelsome discussions finally reached a climax: Half the family would stay, and half would leave. King Solomon would have decided that way, too, I thought, as I remembered his poignant adjudication between two quarreling women claiming ownership of a baby: "Split the baby in half," the King ruled.

Mother asked us to change clothes and put on the winter boots. I sat down to put on the boots and observed Father's pallid face, droopy lips, and vacant stare of his prominent eyes. He stood in the corner of the room, next to the wardrobe chest, drained of all strength, with his shoulders sagging as if carrying a monstrous weight. He looked sad, old, and defeated, and his eyes betrayed fear, as if he had given up all hope.

I became frightened and felt shivers traverse my body. Should I leave Father and Mother like this, I agonized.

"Here, take the two valises I prepared and all the rubles I could find," Mother said as she turned to Luba. "Please take good care of your brother."

Then she hugged Luba and held onto her until she burst into tears. She hugged me, kissed me, her face wet, and said softly, "I love you very much. Remember that, Mehal."

"The angel who redeemed me may bless you," Father whispered as he began Joseph's blessing to his sons that we recited Saturday evenings. He embraced me, his voice hardly audible. Suddenly, as if awakened, he pushed me aside and began to undo the golden chain of his Longines watch, Grandma's wedding gift, from across his vest.

"Here, Mehal, take good care of it," Father said, as he handed me the watch with trembling hands. "It may save your life. And take good care of your sister."

I wanted to tell him that I loved him, but I choked with fright that I might not ever see him again; I could not utter a word. I opened my little valise and carefully packed the watch with the chain. Shortly, Luba and I left our home, joined by six young men with whom she had spoken earlier: Two of them, Hayim and Motel, in their early 20s, were neighbors from across the street; the other four—Joseph, Jacob, Nathan, and David—teenagers from homes further down the street. Hayim had a compass, Motel a map, and we had two flashlights to share. Dusk descended as we hurriedly began walking. We wanted to be as far ahead of the Germans as possible. We also wanted to be far away from our homes, lest we change our minds and turn back. Gripped with fear and guilt, I heard my heart pounding as we began our journey into the dark night and beyond.

Great Synagogue of Dubno

CHAPTER 2

Crossing the Old Soviet Border –

A Step Ahead of the Germans

We headed east on Berka Yoselevicza and then zig-
zagged onto the main thoroughfare, Panienska Street.
The street was clogged with heavy motorized army
equipment heading west: tanks on giant carriers, self-propelled
artillery with long, heavy barrels, armored cars carrying helmeted
soldiers, heavy trucks, and assorted vehicles. There was hardly
room for us to walk, even in single file. Sentries soon forced us off
the paved road. Hayim used his compass to lead us onto a parallel,
narrow, dirt road, heading eastward. We walked for hours on the
road, filled with potholes, through hills and valleys, fields and
forests.

The night was getting darker. A few hours into the night, Luba
began to tire. "My feet are killing me; the shoes are too tight," she
said, nearly in tears. I took her valise to lighten her load and told
her to hold onto me. "Don't go so fast," Luba pleaded.

"If we don't go fast, the Germans will catch up with us," Hayim
countered.

Occasional flares in the distance brightened the sky all around
us, confirming Hayim's concerns. About 2 a.m., exhausted, we
rested in a wooded area, filled with pine trees. The scent of the

pine cones reminded me of the woods near Lublin, where Father had worked as a forester. I stretched out on pine needles with a sweater as a pillow, next to Luba. I heard her and the others fall asleep almost immediately, but I stayed awake. Father's sad eyes haunted me. I felt Mother embracing me, holding me close against her face, moist with tears. "I love you very much, Mehal, remember that," she reassured me. Father and Mother must be so worried and so alone. We should have stayed with them. We should never have left them alone, I thought, full of remorse. Another voice protested: I should have pleaded with them to abandon everything and come with us! I should have! I should have! I felt so guilty.

And Sophie? She might have changed her mind; I should have been more convincing, I should have, I should have…. Distant thumping, like thunder preceding a storm, troubled me; I felt cold and shivered as I began to retrace the day's events. A few hours earlier, I had been with my parents. And now we were alone, running away from home, family, and people we had been raised with. Running where?

"You think you're going on a picnic?" Sophie's warnings echoed in my mind. "Where do you want to go, Mehal? Do you have an address?" I felt good thinking of her, and the thoughts calmed me. I was glad I had been able to see her and tell her I liked her and wanted her to come with us. At last I fell asleep.

I dreamed I saw huge monsters—looking like King Kong I had seen in the movie—surround me and march ever closer towards me. They were angry and threatening. They were so close I could hear them breathe. I wanted to run, but my legs were frozen, I could not move.

We woke at daybreak, as if on command, and went into the woods to relieve ourselves. Luba came back limping. She unlaced her boots and took them off. Her right foot was oozing from a burst blister. She changed her socks and put on her boots again, loosening her laces. We sat down and took out our sandwiches and had our first meal away from home. It felt almost like a picnic, but a picnic it was not, as Sophie had warned. I felt tired and worried. Where were we going? Where were we running? When we were ready to resume our march, Joseph, our neighbor from across the street, spoke up. "Hayim, you seem to be sure of where we're going," he said, "but I'm not. I'm not sure I want to continue walking aimlessly. I'm not sure we can outrun German tanks anyway. And if the Germans come to Dubno, I'd much rather be with my parents."

Nathan joined him, "I think I want to go with Joseph."

"Are you crazy? Don't you hear the thunder of artillery all around? Don't you hear what's going on?" Luba started screaming. "You want to go back and get killed?"

"How do you know we're not going to get killed running away like crazies?"

Joseph shot back. "You think we can run faster than tanks? You think we can run faster than German armored cars? Where are we running to, anyway?"

It was quiet for a moment, and then Luba resumed her pleadings. "We are going to our aunt in Ostrog, and I'm sure she would welcome all of us and let us stay with her. We're already halfway there."

"You talk silly; we're barely a few hours away from home and a few days from Ostrog," Joseph said. "Besides, what makes you think the Germans can't get to Ostrog? Anyway, I hope you can all make it, but I'm going back," Joseph said as he and Nathan left.

The remaining six of us regained our composure and moved on. Hayim reached for the compass in his back pocket. "Oh my

God," he shouted. "The compass is broken! I must have slept on it and crushed its glass."

"Now what are we going to do?" David asked with alarm.

"We'll just have to be more careful. You know, it's easy. In the morning we'll go east, towards the sun, and in the evening away from the sun," Hayim said.

"And what do we do in between and at night?" Luba asked with sarcasm in her voice.

"We'll have to manage," Hayim answered.

We were terribly thirsty. Passing a small farmhouse, we noticed a well but with no pail at the end of the rope. We knocked on the door of the hut. The peasant yelled to his wife, "Don't give anything to the dirty Jews!"

An hour later, we saw a peasant in front of another hut. We explained we wanted to buy water. He agreed. We paid him some rubles, and he brought us a pail, which he attached to the rope wound on the crank of his well. We drank the fresh, chilly water and washed our faces. He also sold us some bread, and exchanged a few words with us. He had an easy smile and kind eyes. Not all Ukrainians are of the same cloth, I thought.

We moved on, walking close to the main road, clogged with vehicles. German planes began strafing the crowded road. We turned north, away from the main road, then east.

It was past noon, and we were hungry. We found some tomatoes that were not quite ripe and cucumbers on a farm near the dirt road. We sat down fatigued, and quietly ate our meager lunch.

After a short rest, we marched through heavily wooded areas and lost our way. Small dirt roads ahead led in several directions, with no sign of which one would take us east. We took a chance on one of them but it led nowhere; we spent a few hours in vain. I wondered if we would ever find our way to Ostrog.

A while later, we stopped at a farm and learned we were going north instead of east. The afternoon sun began to guide us, and we made good progress until dusk. We spent a second night in the woods. As I lay down, I heard the earth's tremors and distant sounds of artillery. I wondered if the German tanks were going to catch up with us, as Joseph had feared.

We got up at dawn and had to move fast. Bursts of artillery grew louder, and I detected a tank in the distance. We had no time to waste. "Not so fast, not so fast," Luba pleaded. Hayim took Luba's valise, and I helped Luba along, particularly up the hills, as we walked. There was no way to mistake our direction; the dirt roads began to fill with other escapees. Late in the afternoon of the second day, we reached the outskirts of Ostrog, 60 kilometers from our home.

The roads were filled with people on foot and carriages drawn by horses or cattle, all streaming eastward towards the old, pre-1939 Russian-Polish border. David also had friends in Ostrog, and our other three companions decided to go with him. We parted, agreeing to meet at an appointed place the next afternoon.

Luba and I hurried towards the home of Aunt Etie and Uncle Sholem. I remembered the way well; I had used it so many times two years earlier, visiting my aunt and uncle, while studying at the *Tarbut*, the Hebrew gymnasium. We reached my aunt's home and knocked on the door. "Come in, come in," Aunt Etie greeted us affectionately, surprised to see us.

Aunt Etie looked much older and shorter than when I had last seen her, two years earlier. In her early 70s, her hair had turned all white, and her face had become full of wrinkles; yet her bluish, sparkling eyes displayed the same vitality, and her gentle smile, the same warmth and softness as before. She made me feel comfortable.

"Sholem, Sholem, come here quickly to meet our important guests!" Aunt Etie exclaimed excitedly. Sholem, my uncle, greeted us effusively with hugs and words of love.

Uncle Sholem seemed to have aged as well in the past two years. Tall, with a narrow frame, he appeared more slender and wiry. His face, with an aquiline nose, thin lips, small brown eyes, and a white, thin beard, conveyed sadness and worry. Wearing a cylindrical *yarmulke* on top of his gray hair, and a dark, long caftan, he looked like the stern *Rebbe* of the *Yeshiva* (religious school) who taught me *Talmud* (commentaries on the Bible).

We sat down at the large table in the middle of the spacious kitchen, which doubled as the dining room.

"How did you get here?" Aunt Etie asked. "What's going on in Dubno? What's going on with the whole family? Come to think of it, let me get you something to drink. Wait until I come back." She returned with hot tea and Luba recounted leaving our parents and spending the last two days on the roads and in the forest between Dubno and Ostrog. Aunt Etie inquired about our grandmother and the rest of the family. Luba spoke for a while but became noticeably tired.

"Enough, Luba, enough," Aunt Etie said. "Let me prepare some hot water for you to wash up."

Shortly, she called us into the bathroom. Luba took off her shoes; her feet were full of blisters.

"Aunt Etie, would you have a couple of bandages?" Luba asked.

"Oh my, oh my, you'll need a lot of soaking and bandages; let me see what I can do," Aunt Etie said. I left Luba and Aunt Etie alone.

An hour or so later, the kitchen table was set for supper. We sat down to eat and resumed our conversation. Later, Aunt Etie took us to a small bedroom. "Here are your beds, children. Sleep well; you deserve a good rest," she said as she left us for the night.

I woke up past noon the next day, my muscles stiff and aching. I went into the kitchen and found Aunt Etie again bandaging Luba's feet.

"Good morning, Mehal, you're finally up, eh? Come, let's sit and have something to eat," Aunt Etie greeted me.

The dining room table, loaded with all sorts of cheeses, sardines, fresh vegetables, fresh bread, and hot oatmeal, looked inviting. I liked it all; I could not stop eating, as we continued our conversation.

A couple of hours later, Aunt Etie and Luba went to clean the dishes, and Uncle Sholem and I moved to the living room and sat down. Uncle wanted to know whether I was still studying the *Talmud.*

"Only once in a while with Father," I said.

He reminisced about my chanting the prayers on Purim, commenting that he liked my voice and my knowledge of the text.

"What do you and Luba want to do if, God forbid, the Germans come here?" he asked.

"We want to cross the border to the Soviet Union," I said.

"And what are you going to do there?" Uncle asked.

"We'll try to find jobs and a place to live. I hope the Soviets treat Jews better than Hitler or even the Poles," I said.

"Did you hear of Stalin's mock trials and executions of Jewish Communist leaders, Jewish poets and writers?"

"No, I didn't," I said.

"We cannot trust anybody," Uncle said. "We can only trust God. He saved us from Haman, and He will save us from Hitler."

I sat quietly and struggled with what Uncle had said. God helped us? Then why had so many of us been killed through the centuries? Why did we now fear for our lives?

Luba rushed into the room, interrupting my thoughts. "Uncle,

Mehal, I'm sorry to break in, but there's bad news. The Germans are on the outskirts of Ostrog. There's panic in the streets. We must leave immediately!"

Aunt Etie joined us and burst into tears. "Where are you going to go, children?" she asked.

"We'll cross the border and go into Russia, as far away as we can," said Luba.

Uncle Sholem and Aunt Etie saw the determination and firm gaze in Luba's eyes. "Go, children, go, if you think you must," Uncle Sholem said. "May God watch over you. Aunt Etie and I are much too old to join you."

"Wait! I'll prepare things for you," said Aunt Etie, as she hurried into the kitchen. She came back soon with wrapped pieces of chicken, some bread, and rubles that she had found. She put everything into our little valises. Luba put on her winter boots and grabbed the bandages Aunt Etie had given her to protect her blisters. We embraced Uncle and Aunt, bidding them goodbye.

Aunt Etie protested, "I will go to the border with you."

"Didn't we agree to meet with David and the rest of the group?" I said to Luba.

"There's no time for that. They are probably gone by now anyway. We must rush; we cannot waste any time."

We left the house and joined an endless stream of men, women, and children heading east towards the pre-1939 Soviet-Polish border. As we drew closer to the border, the streets became clogged. The Soviet guards at the crossing were not letting people through. I was holding onto Aunt Etie, lest she get lost in the crowd. Luba forced her way through to catch up with a small Soviet army truck, and began pleading with the drivers, "Please, can I go with you? Can I go with you?" Their eyes examined Luba, and they smiled to each other. It's the braids, I thought.

"Come on, young comrade," they motioned to her.

"Come on, Mehal, quickly," Luba called.

I sensed the soldiers' disappointment when they saw me join her, but we were on the truck, moving slowly through the crowd. Aunt Etie was following the truck and reciting Psalms. A few times she tripped and got up, tears rolling down her cheeks, all the while praying. I soon lost sight of her as she vanished in the crowd. I felt guilty for leaving them. What was going to happen to her? I became ashamed of abandoning this wonderful old woman and her husband. Shouldn't we have stayed with them? Where are we running to, anyway? I was distraught and frightened.

Minutes later, we were at the border crossing. The soldiers made humorous remarks to the guards about the cute, young lady and her little brother, and the guards let us through. Out of sight of the border, the soldiers turned to us, and in a friendly way explained we should go left, to Slavutka, a village a few kilometers away, where we should be able to find shelter. They had to go in the other direction. We thanked them and started the trek to Slavutka. Soon we were joined by many other lucky people who had been let through the border too.

Darkness fell as we reached a big hall of the Slavutka Gymnasium, filled with escapees. We found a little space along the wall and sat next to our valises. We took out the pieces of chicken and bread Aunt Etie had given us and ate our evening dinner. Then, leaning against the wall, we fell asleep for the night.

Morning came, and we joined a long queue of people waiting for food the town was distributing. Luba went ahead to speak to one of the policemen handing out food. "I'm here with my little brother, and we haven't eaten much. Could you please help us get some food?" she pleaded.

The policeman took a good look at her, smiled and addressed

the crowd with great dignity and pomp. "Comrades! These two children have just come from the other side where they had not had much food in a long, long time. Shouldn't we let them in?"

Surprisingly, people waiting at the head of the queue let us in. We received containers of cabbage soup and slices of black bread, and we sat down on the grass to eat.

Suddenly, Luba got up and began to shout in Polish, "Hey, Leena! Paul! Wait for me, wait for me! Mehal, these are my friends from Rovno; I want to say hello to them," Luba said. She ran off with her valise to see her friends, and I lost sight of them, as the crowd thickened.

"Luba, Luba," I shouted repeatedly, to no avail. The crowds, growing ever larger, engulfed me as an avalanche. Panic-stricken, I worried that this threatening, moving mass of humanity might sweep Luba away with it. I feared the pressing crowd might carry me away as well. I managed to move sideways out of the street and waited for what appeared to me an eternity.

An hour passed, and then I heard Luba's voice. "Mehal, Mehal! Hershl is here, Hershl is here!" I turned around and saw Luba, my cousin Hershl, and a few others coming from the police station, a small wooden building. Hershl and I ran towards each other. He embraced me and held me tight, so I could hardly breathe; he was a strong man. He released me, shivering, as he began sobbing.

"Mehal! Mehal! What a miracle to find you and Luba!"

I was overcome with joy and excitement as well. Hershl, unshaven and disheveled, seemed frightened. His prominent lips trembled, and his light gray eyes were bloodshot and bulging.

I turned to Luba. "Where have you been? I nearly lost my mind looking for you."

"The guards are very nervous here," Luba said quietly. "They heard me speak Polish and took me and my friends into the police station, thinking we were spies or something."

"And Hershl?" I asked.

"Well, you know Hershl, being deaf, likes to talk loud, assuming people won't hear him. This time he talked a bit too loud to his friends in Yiddish, and they all landed in jail as German spies. We better get out of here in a hurry."

Hershl and his companions, half a dozen people who had fled Lutsk ahead of the advancing German armies, looked exhausted, covered with dirt and dust, having been on the road for more than three days. Hershl had been on business in Lutsk at the time, and, not being able to return to his family in Targowicze, fled east. Newlyweds in their early 20s accompanying Hershl appeared particularly distraught, and the young woman on the verge of collapse. Hershl told me the pair had been suddenly separated from family and friends in the midst of their wedding, stricken by panic at Germans marching into Lutsk. The young man, Paul, was tall and slim; his bride, Zhenya, was not much taller than Luba. Zhenya leaned against Paul and held his hand, and Paul, in turn, caressed her dark, long hair, consoling her: "Don't cry my love, it's going to be okay, it's going to be okay."

I turned to Hershl, asking about the rest of the family. "Who knows?" he said turning his eyes towards heaven. "Maybe He knows!"

CHAPTER 3

Making Our Way to Stalingrad –

The Angels of Kirovograd

The whirlwind of war grew ever closer on June 28, 1941, with a cacophony of artillery cannons and Stukkas roaring overhead. The early afternoon sun bore down heavily as Luba, Hershl, the newlyweds, four other friends of Hershl, and I left Slavutka and walked north. Two hours later, we arrived at the Shepetovka railroad station, about 10 kilometers from Slavutka. Echelons at a standstill filled the station, with some locomotives heading west and others, east. Some carried equipment and soldiers to the front, while others overflowed with the wounded, many bandaged head-to-toe, arrayed on stretchers in cattle cars with doors flung open.

People holding bundles and valises, trying desperately to board a train, overflowed the platform. Rifle-bearing soldiers roamed the platform and restrained the crowd from jumping onto the tracks. Because no trains left the station, we became increasingly apprehensive.

Hershl's friends spotted a small, wooded area next to the station, where we hid. We soon launched into a feverish dialogue as to how to proceed. Some of the trains had sentries stationed at the cabooses, while others perched on top of the train's wagons.

37

Our only hope was to jump onto one of the trains heading east, but we feared being shot by the sentries.

Hershl counseled us to wait for a signal, a locomotive's whistle blast, and then make a run for it and jump onto one of the wagons. Others disagreed. Then a locomotive sounded a whistle, and we reacted instinctively the way Hershl had suggested. Luba and I ran towards one of the passenger cars. She reached the steps at the head of the wagon and pulled herself up. I waited until she was secure and then hoisted myself, while the train slowly moved, onto the steps towards the end of the wagon. Hershl, the young couple, and other friends behind me, jumped onto the caboose.

I moved surreptitiously through the open door of the wagon and placed myself and my little valise in the corner next to the open rear. Soon the door of the wagon closed and we were off, at a very slow pace, going east.

Among the wounded, a young, uniformed soldier lay on his back, on the floor along the wall. His neck, torn apart, exposed his trachea, windpipe and part of the chest cavity, filled with blood spurting out with each pulsing of the heart. He choked as if drowning, trying to breathe; his face twisted in agony, and his eyes acquired the sheen of glass. The lips of his half-open mouth tightened as if to scream. He held his hands clenched and his legs stiffly bent at the knees.

An orderly with a Red Cross band on his arm approached the wounded soldier. He knelt down, took out his stethoscope, and listened to the soldier's chest. Then he slowly got up, looked around, pulled a revolver out of his back pocket, put the revolver to the soldier's temple, and fired. The soldier's legs recoiled convulsively, as if pulled by a puppeteer's string, and twitched again and again. His body contorted and tightened. The blood flow diminished, and the soldier lay motionless. The orderly walked away to attend to other wounded.

I stood in the corner, quiet and scared. Not sure whether the orderly saw me, I feared he might notice me and fire his gun again, at me. I had never seen a wounded, bleeding, dying man before. Nauseated, I held back from vomiting with all the power I could muster. "Oh, Lord! What is man? He's just a driven leaf, a passing wind, a flittering dream." I recalled the somber liturgy of the High Holidays and its sorrowful chant, which I had sung as a soloist in the Great Synagogue of Dubno. And what of this young man who had just given his life to fight evil? Would his soul go to heaven? Did he have a soul? Was there a heaven? There was a hell, for sure, and it reigned here, all around!

After a few hours, the train stopped at a small station, and Luba beckoned me into another car. She had managed to make conversation and friends with some of the wounded and the orderlies. I joined her in the corner. While the soldiers were provisioned with rations for dinner, we were handed leftovers— dark bread and some pieces of meat. I felt queasy biting into the meat; I had never eaten non-Kosher meat. Luba noticed my hesitation. "You'll get used to it," she said.

"Where is Hershl? Where are the newlyweds? Where are the others?" Luba asked me.

"They were behind me, and I believe they all jumped on the caboose behind this wagon," I answered.

Luba got up. "I'm going to speak to somebody. Maybe they'll let them in to be with us."

Shortly, Luba, Hershl and his friends, and I jumped into the half-open doors of the cattle car, next to the passenger car Luba and I had been in. Evening descended, and I began to feel more comfortable. The soldiers appeared to be less critically wounded than the ones in the passenger car I had been on. Some of the wounded turned to us, eager to talk. Despite the litany of groans and cries of pain, I somehow managed to fall asleep.

But it was a fitful sleep. The day's events overwhelmed me. The shock of witnessing the agony of the dying soldier brought me face to face with the horrors of the war and the fleetingness of life. I almost lost Luba, I reflected with alarm, and that thought made me feel so tender towards her. Father's words, "Take good care of your sister," took on real meaning. I wanted to protect her, to make sure she would be safe and well. I felt a wave of affection warmly passing my body. Fate willed it that Luba and I be together, that our lives be entwined from now on, and I vowed to guard her well-being.

"Momme," I whispered, "you thought that Luba and I would be away for a day or two or maybe stay with Aunt Etie. We are heading much further east, Momme, destination unknown. Will I ever see you and Tatte? It is scary here, but I'll be brave."

The echelon crawled eastward, often stopping to let through westbound trains, carrying supplies and troops to the front. Two days later, on July 1, 1941, we reached the crowded station at Kiev, the capital of Ukraine.

Radio loudspeakers blared martial music and a voice announced that Marshal Stalin would soon address the Soviet Union.

At noon, everything came to an abrupt silence. Stalin's voice came through the loudspeakers loud and clear. His heavy Georgian accent surprised me. He asserted that the Soviets were heroically repulsing the enemy, and urged those in danger of being overrun by the enemy to burn food, supplies, factories, and warehouses, so as to make the Germans' hold on conquered territory untenable. He went on to extol the greatness of the Soviet Union and its leadership under the Communist Party, and ended with a poignant phrase: "Future historians will surely note Hitler started the war, but Stalin ended it." Everyone burst into applause and began singing the Internationale in tandem with the radio orchestra.

I liked Stalin's speech, particularly his call for people in conquered areas to rise up. It reminded me of Napoleon's invasion of Russia, portrayed in Tolstoy's *War and Peace*, which we had been assigned to read a few months earlier. In 1812, General Kutuzov, then the head of the Russian Army, surprised Napoleon and went on to defeat him, not in battlefield victories, but by sheer attrition, depriving his troops of food and shelter. Now Stalin was employing the same tactics.

The mayhem continued as people were trying to board whatever train they could to escape. Luba had run out to buy food and to fetch water at the station. She returned, accompanied by a handsome young man wearing a lieutenant's hat, oversized, with a red ribbon on its rim; he had a cheerful face, framed by dark hair and lively, dark eyes. Luba introduced him to us as Leonid Michayilvich Kaganovich, and told us he had magnanimously suggested we visit his family in Kirovograd.

"I'll be very thankful if you visit my parents and bring them greetings from me," Leonid said. "I'm sure you will like them; they're wonderful people and will treat you like family."

Overjoyed, we disembarked. Leonid helped us to find a train headed southeast to Kirovograd. Luba, Hershl, the newlyweds, Hershl's other friends, and I boarded the train and bid warm goodbyes to the wonderful Leonid.

We now traveled as ordinary passengers, together with other refugees heading east. Luba brandished a copy of the latest *Pravda*, the official party newspaper she had picked up at the Kiev station, its pages far more explicit than the radio accounts about the war front. As we went on reading, our spirits sank. We did not have a map in front of us, but we knew enough about Poland and about the west European part of the Soviet Union to appreciate the extent of the calamitous Soviet Army retreat. Accounts of the "Southern Front" in particular mentioned the army's withdrawal from Lvov and from the Lutsk-Rovno-Dubno triangle, as well as counterattacks near Shepetovka.

"Shepetovka! That's where we were just two days ago," I exclaimed with horror. "And what about Dubno? The Germans are in Dubno!" The thought horrified me.

We all fell silent, as if in mourning; the fate of my parents, grandmother, aunts, uncles, cousins, and other relatives and friends had been sealed. I slowly awakened to a world forever bereft of home. From now on, Luba, Hershl, and I would be on our own. I spent a restless, sleepless night, full of fear and worry. Later in the day, we arrived in Kirovograd and disembarked and made our way to the home of the Kaganovich household.

We knocked on the door, and a short, dark-haired woman, with some gray patches, welcomed us. Leonid's mother was thrilled to hear about her son, and all too eager to take us into her home. We entered the spacious kitchen, where her husband, a man in his 50s, sat at the table reading a paper. He got up as his wife introduced us and invited us to sit with him and chat. He spoke a beautiful, literary Russian. He knew very little Yiddish, though he boasted that his mother did.

We learned soon enough that Mikhail Alexandrovich and his wife, Neena, were devoted Communist Party members. Mikhail, an engineer, worked as the head of a local factory producing arms; Neena was a financial executive of a meatpacking factory in town. Both well-read, they eagerly corrected mistakes when I showed off reciting some of the poetry of Pushkin and Lematov. Yet, despite their obvious intelligence and education, they appeared ignorant of conditions outside the Soviet Union.

"How did you survive the hunger of the '30s in Poland?" Mikhail asked us. Incredulous, both he and his wife repeatedly questioned our account that we had suffered no food shortages. I remembered reading that the 1930s saw widespread hunger in the Soviet Union, as Stalin forced collectivization of the farms in Ukraine, the "breadbasket" of Europe. It dawned on me that the Communist regime and party would deceptively portray famine as a global phenomenon, certainly one prevailing among the Soviet Union's neighbors.

Neena prepared supper, and we all sat down to eat our first decent meal in a week – she gave us *hors d'oeuvres* with crackers and small pieces of herring, followed by piping hot cabbage soup, then veal cutlets and potatoes. Neena's and Mikhail's generosity and goodness touched me deeply.

They took us throughout their spacious house, consisting of a living room with a piano, a library, two bedrooms, and a large bathroom. Neena was taken by the lovely newlyweds and offered them her own bedroom. "Just for one night. It is your honeymoon!" she exclaimed with a smile. She put Luba, Hershl, and me in the library, and she took the four other friends of Hershl to a neighbor, where they would lodge for a few days. She invited us to wash up and gave us new underwear, insisting that her helper would take care of our laundry in the morning. Soon we retired in the miraculous haven of Eden.

The following week brought us a much-needed bit of rest. While Mikhail and Neena were away working, their helper, a Ukrainian woman, looked after us with great care. Luba, the "bookworm," immersed herself in the library; Hershl and I meandered through the city streets and buttonholed neighbors. The obvious lack of tension or ill-will between the few Jews that we met and the others astounded me. The horror of the war began to recede from my mind, and we felt comfortable. And yet....

In solitude, I found myself bewildered by the frightening, unpredictable changes overtaking my life and the lives of my family and friends. My memory went back to the time when my Gentile classmates began attacking us on our way home, calling us "dirty Jews" and throwing rocks at us. A year earlier we had gotten along quite well. How had I become a "dirty Jew" in such a short time?

How did a young fascist replace my venerable history teacher? How did Poland permit fascists to use corporal punishment against young students? How did Ukrainian churchmen help orchestrate the Jewish pogroms in our town? Why did Father's employer, Zamoyski, fire all the Jews? Why did the University of Warsaw fire Aunt Peshia? So many questions raced through my mind. I faced a monster, anti-Semitism, that drained my strength and cowered me into a midget.

And now Luba and I had turned into vagabonds, homeless, tossed into an ocean of violence and bloodshed. A psychotic killer had turned the world into Jew-hunters, threatening the lives of all Jews, including those of Mother and Father. The thought of this explosive growth of Jew-hating paralyzed me with rage. Had the whole world gone crazy?

"Have you had much anti-Semitism here?" I asked Mikhail Alexandrovich one day.

"No. As you see, Neena and I hold high positions and are well-integrated in the community. We do not practice the Jewish religion, but our passports state that we are Jewish and many in the city know that we are Jewish but don't hold it against us. Nor does Jewish identification, to my knowledge, harm any other Jew in town."

His words impressed me, although I could hardly believe them.

Fearing the fast-advancing Germans, the young newlyweds and other friends of Hershl left Kirovograd. Hershl, Luba, and I remained, enveloped in the goodness of the Kaganovich family.

Hershl and I became closer. Some 20 years older than I, he was the son of my father's oldest of five sisters. He lived with his wife, Celia, and three-year-old son, David, in Targowicze, my father's home village of some 2,000 people, most of whom were Jewish, about 15 kilometers northwest of Dubno. Hershl had visited us often in Dubno, working with my father in the commerce of hops and grain.

Short, stocky with a powerful physique and a round expressive face, brown hair with a tinge of red, Hershl looked like a younger version of my father, except for his unusually large ears. Mother observed that nature had a way of compensating for human infirmity. Hershl had become completely deaf in early childhood when thrown off a horse, an accident that nearly killed him. Emergency surgery had saved him, but not his hearing. Yet he learned to read lips well and he was easy to converse with. We reminisced about my father's five sisters and nephews. The conversation often drifted into Hershl's occasional work with my father. He hugely respected Father's talents as a forester. He admired how Father's easy authority directed hundreds of workers tending the forests under Father's command, without ever raising his voice.

Sunday, July 8, 1941, marked two weeks since we had left home. Mikhail sat in the kitchen reading newspapers talking about the war. He asked me to join him at the table and went on to describe the terrible setbacks of the Soviet army and the loss of all the territories in Poland and the Baltic states that the Soviets had liberated in 1939. He expressed outrage that the Germans were

45

behaving like brutes, murdering innocents, and leaving wounded soldiers to die in the fields.

He opened a newspaper war map outlining the movements of the German army. Three major fronts in the north, center and south stretched along 1,500 kilometers. In the north, the German thrust was towards Leningrad, intended to cut the Soviets from the Baltic Sea; however, Mikhail believed it was of no critical use to the Soviets, since it had been mined. He also believed that the German thrust in the middle, towards Moscow, would not achieve its objective. The Soviet government would probably evacuate all essential buildings, factories, and institutions before the German armies arrived. A deserted Moscow would do no more good to Hitler than it did to Napoleon. The southern theater of war, however, appeared to Mikhail most crucial, since German advances there threatened Ukraine—the breadbasket of the Soviet Union—and the oil riches near the Caspian Sea.

Mikhail further explained that the severe losses suffered by the Soviet army resulted from being unprepared for the surprise German onslaught. He also told me that heavy losses around Lvov were because many Ukrainian officers and some generals were hostile to Stalin and sympathetic to the Germans. Despite the setbacks, Mikhail thought that the Soviets had large reserves and that the Soviet army had begun to slow the German army down.

"I hope we'll be able to stop the Germans. If not in Kiev, then along the Don, and, if not there, then it will be in Stalingrad," Mikhail assured me.

A few days later, Neena returned home early, distraught, and told us that the German forces were moving east of Kiev, bypassing the city. She thought Luba, Hershl, and I should leave. She and Mikhail would like to leave as well, but could not because they held responsible positions in the city, as members of the

Communist Party.

"Where should we go?" Luba asked.

"Go as far east as you can," she answered.

She took Luba by the hand and led her to a sewing machine in the corner of the library. She withdrew colorful pieces of material from the surrounding drawers.

"I will cut the material and give you half to take with you. You should be able to barter the material for bread and other necessities to survive."

The next morning, Mikhail and Neena took us to the railroad station, helped us to obtain travel permits and bought us tickets to Voroshilovograd, a city about 500 kilometers farther east. Neena embraced Luba and the two burst into tears.

"Have a safe trip and don't forget to write," Neena said.

Luba, Hershl, and I boarded the train and left the station. I felt saddened and lonely, without roots, without destination, yet thankful for having met these wonderful people.

Next morning, July 20, 1941, we arrived at the Voroshilovograd station. Single-minded as ever, Luba located City Hall and went to see the director of education to secure a teaching position. The director explained that the city did not have openings in the summer, and suggested she might inquire at a suburb of Voroshilovograd which might need teachers. He offered to give her a letter of recommendation. We quickly headed to the suburb, a small farm town of a few thousand people. The mayor helped us find a room with a middle-aged couple, and he also found a job for Luba in the local factory, which manufactured down jackets for the military. I soon found a job as a letter carrier. But Hershl could not find any work, most likely because he was deaf.

Luba's job turned out to be demanding. The war imposed heavy quotas on the factory to produce large numbers of jackets, in preparation for the winter. She worked ten to twelve hours a day, and often the night shift as well. Always rather fragile, she now turned pale and weak. I worried about her health. Our meager portion of black bread, less than a pound a day per person, and very rare ration of sugar, was all we had to live on, except for the occasional vegetables which the owners of the cottage would give us from the little plot of land surrounding the house.

Hershl surreptitiously found "black markets" where he would barter some of the cloth Neena had given us for some fruit and vegetables. The NKVD (Soviet secret police) would sometimes surround the illegal markets to seek men of military-conscription age, and haul them away.

One day, the NKVD picked up Hershl, along with a dozen other men, and drove them away in a military truck. When Luba and I returned from work, our landlord conveyed the terrifying news. We ran to the local police station.

"Where is our cousin? Where has he gone?" Luba shouted. She explained that Hershl, completely deaf, would do the army no good. Luba's pleadings were to no avail.

The brutal snatching of a completely deaf man, and hauling him away as if he were cattle, horrified me. The pain of parting from my parents was still raw, and Hershl's disappearance exacerbated the gnawing agony. I felt distressed, worrying what would happen to this good man. Would the Soviets send a deaf man to the front? Hershl's disappearance made me painfully aware that Luba and I had been left alone; I was drawn ever closer to her.

My job as a letter carrier ended when a teacher, returning from vacation, volunteered for my position. Soon, however, I landed a job as bookkeeper of the local collective farm. The abacus, the only calculating machine on the farm (and probably in town), became my intimate companion, as I used it to add and multiply columns of numbers with great speed and dexterity.

Town life was poor and primitive. Sundays found everyone washing clothes at the riverbank and hanging them to dry in the sun. Occasionally, someone would catch a fish and all who gathered would celebrate the "feast" by relishing fresh morsels grilled on a bonfire.

The end of August brought harvest time. In addition to working at the office, I volunteered to help on the collective farm, tying up bundles of wheat, digging potatoes, and doing other chores, side-by-side with the farmers and other volunteers. The mood in the evening was particularly friendly and jovial. The young people were fond of singing, and sing they did, harmonizing beautiful Ukrainian and Russian songs, while gorging on roasted potatoes until the early hours of the morning. I joined with the other young people in complete abandon.

Despite the singing and the camaraderie, fear and foreboding seeped into my evenings and nights. Distant earthquake-rumblings, as if from an erupting volcano, echoed far in the darkness of night, occasionally interrupted by bright flares in the skies and bursts of exploding anti-aircraft missiles. My co-workers gleefully shouted, "The Germans are coming, the Germans are coming, and maybe we'll be free at last!"

Their joy shocked me. I understood that they had been torn away from their homes and their own farms and forced to work and live in a communal collective farm, and they hated it. But I knew better. I knew that Hitler's marauding armies would do them far more harm than Stalin had done. The taunting of a young man particularly upset me: "You, Jew, are not so happy, are you? You and your fellow Communists will probably be the first to be shot, ah? Maybe the best you can do is run away."

I seethed with anger that the cancer of anti-Semitism had worked its way across thousands of miles, far from Germany and Poland. Two months earlier, in Kirovograd, Mikhail, completely at-ease as a Jew and a high government official, left me with the impression that anti-Semitism had disappeared in the Soviet Union. Now I had a refresher lesson; I realized that Luba's life and mine were in danger and that we would soon have to flee again.

A few evenings later, I discussed my fears with Luba, who confirmed that she had heard in the factory that the Germans had taken over Kiev and were moving eastward, approaching Voroshilovograd. We decided to leave at daybreak before anyone could see us, since we did not have travel permits.

At dawn we stole out, holding our little valises, one filled with the material Neena had given us, the other with our clothing and some food. Two hours later, we were at the station and repeated the routine we had learned before. We waited until we saw a locomotive hitched to the wagons, and when it blew the whistle, we jumped on one of the open cars. Off we went, heading east.

Two chilly days later, on September 1, 1941, we arrived in Kharkov, where another train, loaded with heavy factory equipment being evacuated to Stalingrad, joined ours. Evacuees from the Kharkov Technical Institute, who filled one of the cars, greeted us warmly and invited us into their covered wagon. They gave us denim jackets and other warm clothing and shared their food with us. The head of the department, a middle-aged engineer, took a particular liking to Luba. It must be the braids, I thought.

The next few days were pleasant, despite the cold and drizzly weather that came all too early that year. Evenings brimmed with new Russian songs, some even referring to Jewish celebrations— on the whole far more sophisticated than the ones I had heard in

Voroshilovograd. We were pleasantly surprised that the department head, as well as most of the faculty, turned out to be Jewish.

Two weeks later, on September 15, 1941, we arrived in Stalingrad, and our new-found friends invited us to go to their assigned quarters, where the Institute was to be relocated. We spent the night on cots in a large room. Towards dawn I heard Luba's voice, quiet but firm, "Leave me alone at once."

"I love you very much, Luba," whispered the department head.

"Get out of here!" Luba replied forcefully. I began coughing and things grew quiet. Apparently the department head complied. In the early morning, Luba turned to me and said, "Mehal, let's go. With friends like these, who needs enemies?" We departed in haste.

Luba found her way again to the municipal education department and asked for work. After all, it was September, and schools were opening. She succeeded in snagging an assignment in Aksai, a small town 70 kilometers south of Stalingrad. We went back to the station and, with new permits in hand, we boarded the train to Aksai.

CHAPTER 4

Surviving, Just Barely, in Aksai –

The Thief

A small farm town of several thousand people, Aksai lay astride the ancient crossroads of Slavs, Mongols, Turks, Georgians, Armenians, and other peoples from the Caucasian region stretching between the Caspian and Black seas. The inhabitants of the town reflected the multi-colored composition of the region's people. Ukrainians of more recent origin added vitality and energy to the area. Stalin's drive to collectivize farms forced the rich farmers of Ukraine, known as the *kulaks*, out of their native habitats, and many of them had settled here. Bitter and hostile, yet hard-working and competent, they were the ones who tilled the ground, raised the cattle, and fed the population. Also notoriously anti-Semitic, they blamed Jewish Communists for their ill fate.

Soon after we arrived, Luba was hired as a teacher of Russian in the local school, and I enrolled as an eleventh grader in that school. I also found a job again as a part-time letter carrier. The school arranged for us to live with a family who owned a small cottage on the outskirts of town, and we negotiated to have a corner of a room with one bed and a chest. The rent took half Luba's salary, which was a pittance, in addition to a portion of our meager rations of bread and sugar, and occasional coal for the stove, which Luba was entitled to receive as a teacher. We also had the privilege of using the stove at off-hours to occasionally boil potatoes or pieces of cabbage and onions. We soon discovered that the family, who had come from Ukraine, resented the regime, and interlaced their conversation with anti-Semitic remarks. When they learned that we were Jewish, they began to show hostility towards us. The woman of the house, often irritable, criticized Luba for trivial matters, or for no reason whatsoever. We persevered, for we had no choice.

October arrived, bringing with it, according to the natives, the coldest weather in their memory. Food became harder to get. Our initial rations of less than a pound of bread per person soon diminished to half a pound; the sugar and other "luxuries" stopped coming, as did the coal Luba was supposed to get. The little money that we had, and even the material that Neena had given us, were of no use, there being no food to buy or barter.

The news of the war continued to be frightening. Radio Moscow's bulletins were terse and fragmentary, but with the help of a map, Luba and I began to construct a picture of the situation. The Red Army continued its retreat on a broad front. In the central theater, the German armies had moved past Smolensk, a key gateway some 300 kilometers from Moscow. In the south, German armies had overrun nearly all of Ukraine, and most of the Don Basin, rich in coal and other natural resources, and were approaching Kharkov.

The newspaper contained bulletins announcing the evacuation from Moscow to the hinterland of governmental ministries, universities, industrial enterprises, and manufacturing plants. I recalled with amazement Mikhail Kaganovich's predictions of such developments during our stay in Kirovograd. "Hitler would find a deserted Moscow of no more use than Napoleon did," Mikhail had concluded with some optimism. However, the thought that the German *Panzer* divisions would sweep across and beyond the very heart of Russia filled me with horror. I began to doubt the Red Army's ability to stop German advances anywhere, if they could not defend Moscow.

In November, the weather became unbearably cold, and snowstorms and drifts made it impossible to go outside for days. Hunger began to ravage our bodies, and my heart would sink looking at an emaciated Luba. I carefully sliced the bread she occasionally managed to bring from school so that she would get most of it, swearing all the while that I had divided the portion equally.

Deteriorating living conditions made the owners of the hut even more irritable and, at times, downright nasty. "Where is the sugar you promised us? Where is the coal you were supposed to give us?" the lady reproached Luba with anger. "You Jews are very smart. You're probably selling it to others, aren't you?" Soon enough, she and her husband asked us to deliver on our promises or leave.

The owners' hostility bewildered me; where did it come from? Where did they learn that the Jews were out to cheat them? They knew full well of the shortage of food and coal in town, and that the school failed to supply teachers with promised necessities.

Luba proceeded to the town hall and pleaded for a new place to stay. The functionaries arranged for us to move to another small cottage with two families, one of which consisted of an older couple and their mentally ill son in his 30s. Evacuees as well, they had lived in the cottage for months. The other residents, the Wieners—a couple, the wife's mother and a young son—originally from Odessa, were in transit to Stalingrad. Norbert Wiener, a

55

rather slight and short middle-aged man with a goatee and penetrating gray eyes, headed a tobacco factory being evacuated from Odessa to Stalingrad. The Wieners grew fond of Luba and helped us get settled.

A week after our arrival, the Wieners' son, Greesha, left for the army, and the Wieners' sorrow spread a pall on the household. Two weeks later, the Wieners departed for Stalingrad.

On December 8, 1941, Radio Moscow broadcast news that Japan had attacked the U.S. Pacific Fleet in Hawaii, and that Washington had declared war on Japan, news that generated great fanfare and ecstatic joy on the radio, as well as in the press. All of a sudden, the United States, considered the strongest nation on earth, had become *de facto*, an ally of the Soviet Union. The future brightened appreciably.

Meanwhile, the radio and newspapers brought encouraging news from the front. The Germans' *Panzer* divisions did come within 20 kilometers of Moscow, but encountered stiff Soviet resistance. In early December, Soviet armies under Gen. Gregory Zhukov mounted a massive offensive against the German armies that encircled Moscow and routed them, capturing many prisoners. On December 13th, *Pravda*, the official Soviet newspaper, boldly proclaimed the defeat and retreat of the German armies around Moscow. This, the first major defeat of the Germans, gave new life and new hope to the Soviet Army and people. Good news streamed in from the southern front as well. General Timoshenko had driven the Germans out of Kharkov, pushing the German armies from the eastern banks of the Don River.

Two weeks after the Wieners' departure, the elderly couple in the cottage died of what was called pneumonia but most likely was starvation. Luckily, the deceased couple left boxes of new clothing, galoshes, and cloth. They also left cartons of coal hidden in a corner. We began to use the coal sparingly on the cold winter nights. Luba helped the young man recover from his mourning and he, appreciatively, drew closer to us. He gave us some material from which Luba ingeniously made warm jackets, which we used to stave off the bitter cold.

I lost my job as a letter carrier, just as I had in Voroshilovograd, the job being too tempting and conspicuous for natives. I began to work after school in the local munitions factory, where the pay was skimpy and the regimen harsh. I labored on a lathe, putting final touches on a metal part for a gun assemblage. We persevered.

A nasty turn of events nearly landed me permanently in jail. We had used up the coal that the young man, our current land-lord, had saved, yet the temperatures at night plummeted, reaching record lows, 30-40 degrees Fahrenheit below zero, and Luba and I suffered frostbitten toes and fingers. Most of the fences were disappearing around town, as people tore them down to burn and provide some relief from the bitter cold.

One night, venturing outside, I found, and took, loose planks from a nearby broken fence. In sheer ecstasy, we broke them into pieces and lit a fire in the stove, which alas, lasted only a few days. In desperation, the next night I walked to search for more wood, and noticed a tree stump on our neighbor's property, lying next to a big pile of timber. As it was too heavy for me to lift, I returned to the house and convinced the young man to go outside and help me get that heavy and awkward stump. Huffing and puffing, we managed to bring it in.

Half an hour later, hearing loud knocks, I opened the door and the silhouette of a tall policeman startled me. "Which one of you hauled in this stump?" he asked angrily.

Luba stepped forward. "I did!"

"Go ahead, lift it, young lady," the policeman commanded, and

Luba being unable to move the stump, he continued, "You see, you shouldn't really mix into men's business." He dismissed the young, retarded man; obviously he was looking for a more suitable victim. He turned to me angrily, "Did you do it?"

"Yes."

"Oh no, I helped him with it. It was all my idea," Luba protested.

"Then you come with me; you're both under arrest."

He took us away in a horse-drawn wagon waiting outside. A few minutes later, he opened the police station door and ushered us in, sending Luba to a room on the left, and me, through a narrow hallway to a small cell on the right. A stench of urine and feces struck me so I could hardly breathe. A pail in the far right corner of the room served as the toilet. On the earthen floor, two men, sharing one blanket, were stretched out next to one another. An orderly gave me a blanket and directed me to lie down in the other corner. I wrapped myself in the urine-smelling blanket and fell asleep.

A few hours later, a policeman awakened me, took me to a small, well-lit office, and ordered me to sit in front of a desk. A slim, wiry man with dark gray hair and penetrating dark eyes came in, dressed in a down jacket. "Good evening," he said harshly. "Your name?"

"Mikhail Moysieyevicz Kesler," I replied.

"Where are you from?"

I told him how we left home, traveling through Ukraine and Stalingrad, and about our short stay in Aksai.

"How did you manage to survive since leaving home? Did your parents give you a lot of money?"

I explained politely the good fortune we had finding the family in Kirovograd, our sojourn in Voroshilovograd, and Luba's work as a teacher, providing food and shelter for both of us. He peppered me with questions for a long time, insisting on knowing if my sister and I had any connections with anybody in Poland or this country. Did I have any instructions or letters to give to anybody? What other languages did I speak? Did I have any connections with Zionists?

Then, unexpectedly, he fired at me, "How much wood did you steal?"

I tried to explain how cold we were and how, in despair, I had hauled in the stump of wood from the next property.

"Did you know it was government property?"

"No, I did not."

"Are you blind? Can't you read the sign? This is the town yard!" he yelled at me. "How many times have you stolen wood from this property?"

"Just the time I told you."

"I have sworn testimony that you stole wood many times before."

Now on the defensive, I apologized. "Three nights earlier, I did pick up two small planks from a fence on the other side of our hut."

"And what did you do before that? How did you survive the cold without a fire of some sort?"

"We used coal that the parents of the man with whom we lived had saved."

"Where are those parents you're talking about?"

"They died about a month ago."

"You're telling me a lot of lies! You've been stealing government wood, using it to burn in your own hut, and selling it to other people as well!" he shouted.

"I didn't do any such thing, sir."

"Let's see how your story is a week or a month from now, as you and your sister rot away here." He shut the file and left the room.

A policeman escorted me to my cell. I woke up bleary-eyed in the morning, to the shouts of my cellmates. "Breakfast is here!" The measly meal consisted of a slice of black bread and hot water. Afterwards, we relieved ourselves in the corner bucket, which an orderly took out and brought back an hour or two later.

I was fearful and distraught. I had told the interrogator everything I knew. What else was he after? And what was happening to Luba? Where was she? The questions kept bombarding me, like bees gone mad out of a beehive. What were they accusing me of? Would we ever be released?

A few months before, I had been completely immersed in the school's required reading of *Les Miserables*. Was I going to suffer the same fate as Jean Valjean, who ended up in forced labor on an island near France? Would I land in a camp in Siberia? He had stolen a loaf of bread; I, a useless stump of wood. Anyway, how do you make a fire out of a stump of wood without an axe or a saw?

I remembered the anti-Semitic taunts of the young man in Voroshilovograd who reminded me threateningly that I was a Jew, and that the Germans would soon take good care of the likes of me. The jeering remarks of the homeowner lady where we had stayed earlier in Aksai, "You're Jewish, so you must have sold your rations. You Jews are very clever, aren't you?" came to my mind, as did the nasty questions of this latest inquisitor, about my Jewishness and Zionist connections.

As the day wore on, one cellmate was taken away, and I was left with the remaining one, obviously half-witted. I wrapped myself in the dirty blanket to stop shivering, and fell asleep. Later, an elderly woman brought watery cabbage soup and a piece of black bread. The monotony of the day wore on. Where is Luba, where is Luba rang in my mind. Why had she come forward saying she helped me bring in the wood? It was unlikely that would help me anyway. Evening brought another watery portion of cabbage soup, and I fell asleep.

I awoke and felt guilty and ashamed of committing thievery. Would Father have approved of my stealing wood? The voice of the *Rebbe* (teacher) at the *Yeshiva* (Hebrew school) I had attended in Dubno, came to my mind: "Saving a person's life takes priority over everything else, including observance of the laws of the Sabbath." By extension, this teaching would apply also to the commandment "Thou shall not steal," I reflected. The bitter cold endangered our lives, and certainly jeopardized Luba's health. I became convinced that Father would understand that. Would the interrogator understand my predicament?

Long past midnight, a policeman took me to the room where I had been interrogated the night before.

The same hard-bitten officer was at it again. "So how did you arrange to steal so much wood?"

"I only took in one stump of wood," I replied.

"And what about the other planks that you admitted to stealing earlier?" he exclaimed triumphantly.

"The other planks, sir, were from the fence on a different property."

"Look, we're talking about a lot of wood that has been stolen from government property. You better understand the seriousness of the charges, and stop giving me false, childish answers. Whom have you been working with? Who are your friends here, and who are your sister's friends?"

I denied having any friends. The officer began to shuffle his papers, and remained quiet for a while. "Mehal, your sister has confessed that you stole a lot of wood. Either she is lying, and she will pay for it dearly, or you are lying. Be sure of one thing, neither your sister nor you will leave this place until you tell us the whole truth. I want to know who your accomplices are. Who have you and your sister worked with to steal all that wood from government property?" the inquisitor bellowed.

"I'm telling the whole truth, and I don't believe that my sister confessed to anything else. She's not a liar, and she would not tell things that aren't true."

My answer enraged him. He stunned me as he slapped me in the face with all his force. "You're accusing me of lying? Do you know what you're doing? You're offending a government official. Such an offense carries heavy punishment!"

"Sir, I don't mean to offend you, but I know my sister."

"Well, well, you're a stubborn young man, aren't you? We shall see what the truth is."

With that he left, and a policeman took me back to my cell. I trembled with fear: what on earth did he want to get out of me? To invent other stories, more to his liking, would plunge me in bigger trouble. I knew for sure that Luba would not invent lies either, unless they tortured her, or threatened to hurt me.

The third day came, and brought no relief and no hope. I began to walk around the cell like a caged animal that I had seen in the Ostrog Zoo. Cold and hungry, I was out of my wits. Not a word from Luba or about Luba, and no one to talk to, except for the half-witted man. The stench of the bucket full of urine and waste filled my nostrils and penetrated my whole being. "Luba! Luba!" I began shouting, seething with anger.

The third night arrived, and around midnight, I again faced my inquisitor. "I have prepared a summary of my interviews with you. You can look through it quickly and sign it," he said.

With sleepy, bleary eyes, I leafed through pages of things that I had never said, among them a confession that I stole, on numerous occasions, large quantities of government property. I was shocked and puzzled.

"Sign it," he commanded, "and I'll let you go."

"But…" I began to protest.

"Spare me your excuses. If you don't sign it now, you'll sign it tomorrow, or a week later, or a month later. Sign it and stop being foolish."

"Will you let my sister go?"

"Only if you sign," he answered. I felt I had no choice, and I signed the document.

In the morning I was released. I returned to our place, and found Luba there crying. "I've worried about you so much," she sobbed.

"What happened to you, Luba?" I asked, embracing her.

Luba told me she was released the next morning. Her high school principal had noticed her absence and, fearing she might have been arrested, went to the police. Learning she was jailed, he became angry and demanded her release. He told the police they had no right to arrest anybody for getting wood to heat their huts in this bitter-cold weather. "Do you want my teachers to freeze to death?" he shouted, recounting the incident to Luba.

"They released me, but they were really set on nailing you as the prime suspect," Luba concluded. "Now tell me what happened to you."

I told Luba about the midnight interrogations, the miserable jail cell conditions, the inquisitor's fabrications that she had confessed, and the papers he made me sign.

"What did you sign, Mehal?" she asked with alarm. I told her, and her face turned ashen. "That confession will probably land you in Siberia all right and I just hope I'll be able to join you." She burst into tears.

My trial, having been set for early March, we spent the next two months searching for a lawyer to defend me of a crime more serious than I could imagine. A woman, a senior member of the local Communist Party, ran the government property adjacent to our hut, and she filed an affidavit attached to my case, stating that she was missing two truckloads of wood, telephone poles, and an assortment of wood for bridges and other strategic uses. Her affidavit named me as the prime suspect in the case.

In early February 1942, a veterinary school, evacuating from Moscow to Aksai, offered courses in the evening. I immediately quit my work in the munitions factory and enrolled to train as a veterinary assistant. Meanwhile, we both became immersed in preparing for my trial. We desperately tried, but failed, to find a lawyer who would defend my case. One lawyer explained to us that the Aksai judge, prone to handing out severe sentences, would show me no sympathy, considering my written confession. The Soviet Union heavily punished theft of government property. He feared that I might be sentenced to spend some time in a labor camp in Siberia.

Two weeks before the trial, my outlook brightened. A prominent Jewish lawyer from Stalingrad arrived to prepare the defense of a major criminal case to be tried in Aksai. Luba managed to see him and pleaded that he take my case. Her good looks (and braids) and persuasiveness with people made the difference; the lawyer agreed to defend me, without pay.

Early in March, Luba and I, and the "angel" lawyer walked into the small courthouse. We soon learned that the trial would be judged by three citizens, not the Aksai judge. Furthermore, the chief prosecutor, a rabid anti-Semite, had other business to attend to in Stalingrad. The assistant prosecutor, a young, mild-mannered man, would instead present the case. Two middle-aged women and one man sat on the dais. Luba spotted my high school teacher and her good friend, who had come to testify on my behalf.

The young prosecutor demanded the court pass a severe sentence to discourage stealing government property, particularly by guests of the Soviet Union. Then he called our neighbor, the woman who had filed the affidavit, to testify about the enormity of my crime. According to her report, she was missing two truckloads of valuable wood, some of it destined as building materials for the front, and I had admitted stealing it.

Then came the defense's turn. First, my lawyer called the high school teacher to the witness stand. She testified that I was the best student in the eleventh grade, probably the best in the high school, and that I was a quiet, affable young man, a model for other students, working hard under severe conditions to excel in every subject. She also volunteered that the high school never gave her the coal that she was entitled to as a teacher. Then she turned to the judges and suggested that Aksai looked eerie with absolutely no fences left. People were forced to use that wood to survive through the cold.

The next witness was the principal of the school, whose presence startled Luba and me. He confirmed that the school was supposed to give coal to its teachers, but that none was available. Luba, the sister of the accused, was certainly entitled to have coal to keep from freezing in this terrible winter, and he could understand how desperate her brother was to provide some means of warming up their place.

Then my lawyer turned to the woman who had filed the affidavit and asked who made up her inventory of the wood delivered, goods sold, and goods remaining in the yard.

"I did," she replied.

"Did you have anybody else help you in this effort?" my lawyer continued.

"No, I did it by myself."

During closing testimony, my lawyer appealed especially to the two women who had sat quietly during the trial, one of them wiping tears from her face during the teacher's testimony about me.

"Honored judges! These two young people fled their homes ahead of the Germans and miraculously survived their long ordeal of coming here to Aksai to live among you. The young man, an exemplary student, works afternoons to learn a new vocation. His sister is teaching your children. These wonderful young people want to live and do well for themselves and for the community. The community owes them minimum means to survive the winter, a minimum of food, some shelter, and the barest amount of wood or coal to prevent them from freezing. The community has failed them. The young man ran out at night, in desperation, to fetch a piece of wood, so as to keep his sister and himself from freezing to death. The story of this young man stealing two truckloads of wood has been concocted to cover somebody else's crimes. This young man and his sister have suffered enough the last two months, first locked in jail, and then living in fear of being convicted. It is time to exonerate the young man."

The court was dismissed. Luba and I ran over to the lawyer to thank him profusely. The decision of the court arrived two days later. I was given six months' probation. Luba and I could breathe freely again.

Spring 1942 brought with it somewhat larger rations of bread, and shorter queues for other necessities. I found my schoolwork easy, and I began to devote much more time to my veterinary courses.

Farm visits, animal inspections, and interviews with farmers supplemented anatomy lectures and courses of local-animal diseases. Once, we helped a cow deliver a calf by pulling the calf's feet with all the force we could muster. I found the event difficult, though fascinating, as we watched the mother affectionately lick her new offspring.

At the end of June 1942, I completed the eleventh grade of high school, as well as my formal veterinary course. However, my veterinary training continued, because the Institute sent me to a farm a few kilometers from Aksai to do my internship with an experienced veterinary assistant who became my mentor. We went from farm to farm, inspecting cattle for any sign of infectious disease. We also attended to any day-to-day problems, such as injuries or health problems farmers would discuss.

The collective farm gave me a horse, and I got my first experience with long hours of horseback riding, which proved to be much fun, but also quite painful for the back and the rear. I became the proud keeper of a small room, with a little wood stove, and a couple of pots, which I could use to prepare simple meals, mostly of potatoes and cabbage.

In mid-July, while visiting Luba in Aksai, she told me she had gone to Stalingrad the preceding week and spent a few days with the Wieners. They lived in a spacious apartment and were waiting for personnel and equipment from the tobacco factory he headed in Odessa to arrive and be transported across the Volga. Then she described an incident that left me worried.

Wiener stored, in his apartment, a lot of tobacco that he had stolen from the factory. Tobacco being a rare and precious commodity in Stalingrad, Wiener probably had intended to sell it. Apparently one of the workers had betrayed him, and Wiener was concerned the NKVD might search his apartment, and, finding the tobacco, would certainly arrest him. Luba offered to help him.

She wrapped herself with a lot of tobacco leaves, tied them with a rope, put on Mrs. Wiener's old raincoat, and surreptitiously left the building. Later in the day, Mr. Wiener met her in an abandoned warehouse, and he retrieved the tobacco, full of thankfulness to Luba.

"Luba, Luba, how did you dare do such a thing?" I shouted. "The NKVD could have apprehended you, and you would have suffered the same fate as Mr. Wiener. How can you jeopardize your life like that?"

"Hush, don't worry so much, I'll be okay," she assured me, as she embraced me.

Luba continued her account of the visit. While in Stalingrad, she learned that a school in telecommunications, evacuated from Leningrad, was en route to Tashkent and was looking for students to sign up. Luba registered to study in that school, hoping that she would be free to go to Tashkent as a student. "If you behave, I'm going to take you with me," she teased.

Meanwhile, news from the ubiquitous Radio Moscow, as well as from the latest *Pravda* Luba had brought with her from Stalingrad, turned worrisome. The Germans did pull their forces from Moscow, but shifted them to the southern front. Refreshed with new supplies of personnel and arms, they began an ominous thrust towards Stalingrad. They had overrun the Crimea and Sevastopol, crossed the Don River, conquered Kharkov, and were approaching Rostov. The Soviet armies, in disarray, were retreating on a broad front.

The thumping, thunderous volleys of artillery, as well as bright flares of anti-aircraft, awakened me at night. Fear of impending disaster overshadowed all else. It seemed as if the new German offensive was inflicting on Soviets the same disastrous blows as it had during the first weeks of the war.

A few days after the conversation with Luba, in early August 1942, I saw her in the distance while I was riding my horse. Yes, it was she: I recognized her silhouette, the braids swaying to and fro, as she walked along the dirt road. I commanded my horse to trot, and I was soon with her. She carried a heavy bundle and looked quite tired and worried. I got off my horse and embraced her.

"Mehal, we must leave immediately," Luba said. "The Germans are approaching Stalingrad and are tightening a noose around the city. I have all of my possessions in this sack, but there's much to do before we can leave. Let's go to your place."

I took the bundle from Luba in one hand and carried the horse's reins in the other. Luba, walking beside me, reminded me that I was still on probation and could not move. She had learned that the head of the local garrison had his headquarters nearby, and she decided to plead with him to give me a permit to leave. I was startled, but I had come to trust Luba's judgment.

Luba advised me to take Father's watch with me, and we took off to see the colonel. Approaching the shack, Luba asked that I detach and give her the golden chain of the Longines watch. Then she went inside. A while later, she came out, beaming. "I've got your permit, Mehal. Now let's go back to your shack." I took my horse to the farm center and explained to the assistant chieftain that I was leaving, showing him my permit. He read it carefully, then shook my hand and wished me good luck. I returned to my shack, picked up my few belongings, and left with Luba.

We headed as fast as we could towards the Aksai train station. I turned to Luba and asked how she had convinced the colonel to give her the permit. Luba told me that she described to the colonel our precarious situation, how she feared we would be killed, as Jews, if the Germans conquered Aksai. She showed him her admission papers to the Telecommunications Institute and implored him to issue a permit to enable me to join her in Tashkent. He hesitated, but Luba put the golden watch chain on his desk. She explained that when we left our home, Father had given us the golden chain, expressing a wish that it might save our lives, and that we would be delighted if he would accept that gift, since the permit might, indeed, save our lives.

Soon we reached the train station and spotted a single train with a locomotive attached to it. We knew our routine well. We waited until the locomotive blew its shrieking whistle and then jumped onto the train's caboose.

Once we were settled, Luba asked me for the watch. She opened her bundle and found a long string, which she tied around the hook of the watch, securing the other end through the buttonhole of my shirt pocket. "I think the watch will be safer now," she said.

A few hours later, as dusk began descending, on August 12, 1942, the train pulled into the Stalingrad railroad yard, filled with trains and jarred by commotion. We jumped off the caboose and ran across the tracks, past the parked trains, toward the railroad station.

CHAPTER 5

Fleeing Stalingrad – The Watch

Volga, Volga Russian River
Volga, Volga Mother Dear
Accept a gift from your humble givers
A Don Cossack and his peers.
(A Russian folksong)

Panicked men and women seeking escape filled the Stalingrad train station. A wave of despair spread through the huge hall as the PA system announced, "No more trains to the south."

I exclaimed to Luba in disbelief, "So, our train from Aksai must have been the last one, wasn't it?"

She agreed, but urged me to hurry so we could reach the Wieners before it became dark.

Military traffic clogged the streets, with soldiers crowding each corner. I could sense an air of crisis gripping the city. People hurried to get wherever they were heading. Long queues were forming at places that handed out rations. Finally, we reached the apartment house where the Wieners resided, and the doorman waved us in.

Luba knocked on the door. Mrs. Wiener opened it and shouted in disbelief, "Norbert! Look who's here!"

She embraced Luba as if she were her own daughter; I could see she was very fond of Luba. Mr. Wiener came over, hugged Luba, shook my hand, and led us to the living room.

"Sit down, rest a bit," Mrs. Wiener said. "Let me bring in Mother. She'd love to see you."

Mrs. Wiener went out and came back with the old woman. "Mother, you remember Luba and Meesha from Aksai?" The woman embraced Luba as she sat down and joined in the conversation.

Luba recounted our escape from Aksai, how she orchestrated getting the permit from the garrison commander for me to travel to Tashkent, and how we managed to get on the last train leaving Aksai for Stalingrad. Then she asked whether the Wieners had heard from their son, Greesha.

"Not a word," Mr. Wiener answered with a sigh. Profoundly worried, he did not know whether his son was even alive. "This latest German offensive is so vicious; we've lost so many people. Who knows? We console ourselves by blaming our mail system that has collapsed with the war. And what about Hershl?" he asked.

His inquiry startled me; Luba must have told the Wieners on her last visit of Hershl's disappearance in Voroshilovograd. Luba told Mr. Wiener that she had inquired with various military units as to his whereabouts, but had received no reply.

Mrs. Wiener asked us to wash up and come to the dining room. We sat at the dinner table, and Mr. Wiener soon expressed concern about the situation in the city. It appeared that the Germans and its vassal armies, several million strong, were encircling Stalingrad.

"What do you think we should do?" Luba asked.

"I believe you should leave the city as soon as you can," Mr.

Wiener replied. "I wish Zhenya, our mother, and I could leave. But I have to stay with the factory until I'm told to go, and I don't know if, and when, this will happen."

We retired to our bedroom. As the night wore on, the shriek of artillery shells, the roar of aircraft bombardment, the hiss of anti-aircraft fire bursting in the air, and the wail of sirens of the emergency vehicles continued unabated. Flares lit up the sky, as if it were broad daylight. The terror of the night made me fear that the world around me would soon be aflame, and engulf the Wieners, Luba and me.

Morning came, and we all sat in the kitchen for breakfast. Mr. Wiener looked more distracted and nervous than he had the evening before. "I just listened to the news, and I'm very concerned for you," he told us. "I heard about a ship that will be leaving towards Astrakhan on the Caspian Sea. One of you should stand in line and try to get tickets to board that ship." He got up and embraced Luba, bid me good luck, said goodbye to Zhenya and her mother, and left.

I found a long queue of people waiting to get tickets for the ship. I joined the line as more and more people filled the narrow street leading to the docks. Hours went by and the line crawled.

The early August sun left us hot and dizzy. I felt as if I were being carried along by the surging crowd. I leaned against the arms of a tall man. Sweaty, thirsty, tired, I closed my eyes just for a moment to relax and dozed off. Jarred by a violent jerk and the tearing of the shirt pocket that held the watch, I saw a lean, short teenager running away. I jumped out of the queue and began chasing the teenager who, faster than I, melted into the crowd.

I despaired: this had been the most important possession Luba and I had. The watch was the last thing Father had given me when we parted, and his words rang in my ears. "Take good care of this

73

watch, Mehal. It may save your life one day." Now I had lost it; I felt angry and disappointed with myself.

I saw no way to rejoin the queue, now blocked by policemen. Slowly, sadly, I returned to the Wieners. Luba, who was waiting for me, sensed something was wrong, and when I explained what happened, she turned livid. "How could you do such a thing? Why didn't you rejoin the queue right away? Who knows whether we'll have another chance to cross the Volga? The radio just announced Stalin's order forbidding anyone to leave Stalingrad. He wants everybody to defend the city."

I felt sorry for Luba, as well as for myself. The day wore on. Mrs. Wiener consoled me. "Don't worry. There will probably be another ship tomorrow, and you'll be able to buy tickets to leave."

In the evening, Mr. Wiener heard what had happened to my watch and suggested we wait until he got his permit and join him and his family when they left Stalingrad.

The next morning, Luba fetched a few things for Mrs. Wiener, and returned with the local newspaper, whose huge front-page headlines brought stunning news: "Ship Hits Mine, All Perish." The paper identified the ship as one carrying a few hundred passengers towards Astrakhan on the Caspian Sea. The news stunned us into silence.

"Sorry, Mehal, I should not have yelled at you yesterday," Luba said, embracing me with tears in her eyes. Chills shot through my body, as I remembered Father handing over the watch to me with trembling hands, just before we parted. Did Father's prayers prevail so that the watch saved our lives, or was it just an accident? Perhaps Father was watching over us, I reflected, bewildered.

The city took on an eerie feeling, day by day. At night, all lights had to be turned off, and the streets became dark and vacant. New ordinances urged people to avoid any unnecessary travel to

74

conserve fuel, to store food, and to secure shelters. Residents of neighborhoods were mobilized to dig ditches and to scatter abandoned trucks, carriages, and metal equipment of any kind, for anti-tank defense.

The nights reverberated with the din of artillery, aircraft, and exploding bombs. I felt that the spasms of deafening eruptions were tearing the city's innards, and I imagined they would lift the earth's mantle, swallowing us all into the gaping void. I trembled as I remembered the day Luba and I left home with the ominous foreboding of never seeing our parents again.

I shared my feelings with Mr. Wiener, who expressed his concerns as well. "What you see, Meesha, is the beginning of the battle of the century, and whoever prevails in this will surely win the war. It's like watching two giant gladiators fighting it out on a tightrope held by fate; one misstep, and one of the gladiators will fall into the abyss. But we must not lose faith. The Germans may have the superiority of arms and men, but we have the will. The Germans may retreat if they don't succeed, but we have no place to retreat to." Then Mr. Wiener revealed that Stalin made major changes in the Red Army's leadership, assigning Gregory Zhukov, the Moscow defender, to take over the command of Stalingrad's defense.

That night, I dreamed of the children of Israel at the edge of the Red Sea, with the water in front and the Egyptian army closing in on them. Panic-stricken, they cried out for help. Then the huge, strong figure of Moses appeared, glowing in the darkness, as he stretched his hands over the sea. "Follow me," he shouted, and as the multitude moved forward, the sea parted, and the Israelites passed through, between two frozen walls of water, reaching the other shore. I woke up in awe and wondered: Will the people of Stalingrad and its Soviet Army defenders be able to cross the mighty Volga? And who will be the new Moses to save them?

The news on the radio or in the local newspapers did not reveal much, but word-of-mouth, like electricity in a wire, traveled fast. It became clear that the Germans were tightening their grip on the city, day by day.

One evening, towards the end of August 1942, Mr. Wiener announced that we would be leaving town by horse and wagon, and board a small boat to cross the Volga. Zhenya had already been prepared for it, and two hours later, we left the apartment building, one by one. We met at a corner a few blocks away and mounted our horse-drawn carriage. Half an hour later, we arrived at the riverbank. Soon, a small boat docked, and we descended into its hull. "We must be quiet, and we must be lucky; this is a dangerous trip," Mr. Wiener whispered. Two oarsmen propelled the boat away from the shore and onto the river. I wondered how they knew to avoid mines of the kind that blew up the ship which we had intended to board two weeks earlier. A few hours later, we reached the eastern bank of the mighty Volga, seven or eight kilometers away. Mr. Wiener paid the captain a handsome sum of money, and then arranged for our safe passage on dry land as well. We stayed in a small hut, and in the morning, we boarded a train heading east.

Safe, traveling in a comfortable passenger car with a modest supply of food, I felt relieved, as if released from a hermetically sealed vessel under monstrous pressure. The train moved slowly, often stopping to let westward-bound military supply trains and soldiers pass. We traveled through endless vistas of nothingness, with no visible sign of life for hours on end.

Occasionally, we would stop at small stations where local women with dark, long hair and Mongolian features greeted us, carrying flatbreads, fruit, and drinks.

One day, Mr. Wiener motioned me to his compartment and closed the door. "Sit down, Meesha," he said. "Luba told me about your terrible experience in Aksai, fearing you'd be sent away to Siberia. Join the crowd!" He burst out laughing. "I, too, have feared many times being sent away. So have many millions in the Soviet Union. How else can one feed a family? How else can one survive here?"

He told me of the harsh life in the Soviet Union, how salaries were inadequate to live on, and how one had to scheme to feed a family, often risking apprehension by the secret police. Most business was conducted by barter, under the table, conditions which had prevailed even in peacetime.

When he asked about my life in Poland, I explained that anti-Semitism was the biggest problem in my hometown plus the constant fear of pogroms and schoolyard assaults. "Anti-Semitism has no boundaries and no dateline," he said. "We have written in our passports that we are Hebrew, Jewish, but we can hardly practice our religion or culture." He expatiated about Soviet show trials of the best of Jewish writers and poets in the mid-30s, and of their executions for crimes they had never committed.

Mr. Wiener wanted to know about the life of workers in Poland. My mention of frequent strikes in factories animated him. He explained that workers did not have the right to strike in the Soviet Union, regardless of how poorly they're paid or treated. The regime guaranteed workers the freedom of puppets dancing on strings pulled by members of the Communist Party, largely incompetent, corrupt people. Flushed with excitement, with beads of sweat running down his face, he appeared uncomfortable, as if regretting all he had said.

His words shocked me. I remembered the impromptu views of

Mikhail Kaganovich in Kirovograd, which conveyed so much enthusiasm about the Soviet system. However, Kaganovich belonged to the Communist Party, while Wiener did not. But Wiener's views resonated much more truly with me, particularly since my experience in Aksai.

Three weeks after leaving Stalingrad, the train stopped at a key station. One track led south towards Uzbekistan, the other toward Chkalov in Southern Siberia, where Mr. Wiener's factory was being relocated. Luba's papers, as well as mine, compelled us to head towards Tashkent. Sadly, we had to part with the Wieners. I stood stoically as Zhenya and her mother embraced me with wet cheeks; Luba choked back tears, too. Mr. Wiener gave me a handful of rubles and said, "I know this money may not be worth much, but who knows," as he shook my hand.

The Wieners' wagon separated from our train, as another locomotive came to fetch them. We moved to an empty train wagon to continue our journey. The emptiness of the wagon, the monotonous clatter of the wheels, and the endless naked terrain put me in a trance. I pictured being back at home basking in Mother's love. With Father being away for weeks as a forester, working for the Soviet government, and Luba studying in distant Rovno, Mother showered all her attention on me. Evenings and on weekends, she would read in Russian, volumes of her favorite poets, Pushkin and Lematov, as well as Schiller and Heine in translation.

Henry, my closest friend, appeared before me, as in a dream, while we perused new issues of Soviet scientific periodicals. We devoured articles by Kapitsa and other Soviet scientists dealing with developments in 3-D visualization, in cryogenic temperatures approaching absolute zero when all internal motion of materials came to a standstill and resistance to electric current disappeared. We dreamed to be scientists someday and discover cures for cancer.

Teenage years are wonderful for dreaming. It is a time when one tastes the first few bites of the apple of knowledge Adam and Eve were tempted by in paradise. Intoxicated by Soviet propaganda, we had paid no attention to the approaching storm. Dubno, my hometown, sat on the banks of the lazy Ikva River, quiet, relaxed, as if half asleep; and so were its Jews, fearful, yet hoping that all would turn out well.

My father was a good man, gentle, kind, and peaceful. Mother would often berate him as a dreamer, a naïve dreamer. He loved his profession. Working in the woods gave him an inner peace and a firm belief that God created a beautiful world for people to enjoy and exploit. Descending from a family of rabbis and scholars, he conveyed to my sister and me a zeal for being good and doing good, for being fair and honest. None of his teachings, nor of my mother's love, appeared to matter now.

The world around me was severe and empty, devoid of any context. The wheels' clickety-clack indicated we were on the move, but where to? I had no sense of what waited for us at the end of the train ride. I had no dreams and no desire to dream. I no longer felt as a teenager. The events in Aksai, where I nearly had been sent to Siberia, the frightening picture of the thief running away with my watch, and Mr. Wiener's exposition of the harsh life in the Soviet Union, had made me feel much older. I must grow up, I whispered to myself. Luba and I have been thrown into a jungle surrounded by vicious war. I must learn to fight. I must take care of Luba....

A few days later, on September 25, 1942, we arrived in Tashkent. The railroad station overflowed with variegated people, poly-glottal and poly-garbed, most of whom were Jewish refugees who held onto their meager bundles. A great mixture of colorfully robed and curiously head-geared people with slanted dark eyes, straight dark hair, and facial expressions reminded me of Mongolian tribes I had seen in my well-thumbed history books.

We left the station and headed towards City Hall, which we found closed. The park across the street brimmed with refugees, just like us. We rested our bundles on a grass plot and fell asleep as evening descended. A sudden jerk of my bundle woke me. I saw two teenagers about to run away with it. I had a flashback of the fellow in Stalingrad who stole my watch while I stood in the queue for a permit to cross the Volga. This time, I ran faster than they did. I slugged one with all the force I could muster, grabbed my bundle, and started kicking the other teenager, as people came to my rescue. I came back to Luba and found her holding onto her bundle, crying out for help.

In the morning, Luba enrolled as a student at the Telecommunications Institute, where she had registered a few months earlier in Stalingrad. Since the Institute did not provide housing, we headed to the marketplace to seek people's advice about where to find a place to stay. Milling around in the market, I noticed Luba startled, turning to a woman tugging her braids.

"Neena!" Luba cried in astonishment. She embraced our angel lady from Kirovograd.

"What a miracle it is to find you here!" Neena Kaganovich exclaimed.

She was grayer, and a bit more stooped than I remembered her a year earlier. She and her husband occupied an apartment nearby, she told us. When Luba explained our situation, Neena instantly volunteered, "Luba and Meesha, you come with me; you'll stay with us." She said it with such enthusiasm that we could not refuse.

We walked with Neena to a tall building and climbed three flights of stairs, whereupon Neena opened the door of an apartment at the end of a long, narrow hallway. In the kitchen sat Mikhail Alexandrovich, looking considerably older and grayer, far more subdued and sadder than when I had seen him last.

"Let me take you through the grand living quarters," Neena said sarcastically, as she took me and Luba by the hand.

Their apartment consisted of one small bedroom, a living room—more like a hallway—a kitchenette, and a bathroom. Neena pointed grandly to the living room.

"This will be your palatial suite," she said with a smile.

We placed our bundles on the small couch and went back to the kitchenette. The Kaganoviches had departed Kirovograd a few weeks after we had left, and then sojourned in Kharkov with relatives until forced to flee. They had come to Tashkent two months ago and were still looking for employment.

"Have you heard from Leonid?" I asked.

"Not a word," Neena answered. "We haven't gotten any letters since the day you brought us his letter from Kiev, and we don't know whether he is even alive. We have written so many letters to various military officers, inquiring about our son, but we never get an answer. And where is Hershl?" she asked. Luba explained how Hershl had disappeared in Voroshilovograd, and we lost touch with him.

The news of the disappearance of Leonid, like the news I had heard earlier of the disappearance of the Wieners' son, Greesha, struck me with horror. How could young people serving their country in the armed forces disappear without a trace, without any letters or notices to their families? Sure, a war was raging, and yet the unsettled conditions made it especially important to let families know where their sons were.

During the meal Neena prepared, mostly of local vegetables, I reminded Mikhail that, when we were in Kirovograd, he had predicted the Germans' onslaught on Stalingrad, and that the Soviets would repulse the Germans. Much more subdued now, Mikhail gave me a brief summary of the year's developments in the war.

He had been more optimistic towards the end of last year, when Zhukov repulsed the Germans near Moscow, Mikhail explained. Since then, Zhukov had been confined to the Moscow area. Stavka, the political arm of the Defense Department under Stalin, had been in command of the fighting, and had not done so well. A number of offenses by the Red Army during the winter months, along the 1,500-kilometer front, had led to great losses.

Meanwhile, the Germans began, in the spring, a massive offensive in the south, and were able to advance to Stalingrad. Mikhail still felt that the Soviets had tremendous reserves in the hinterland, which would stand them in good stead. He still believed in the Soviet Union's supremacy and was particularly enthusiastic about Zhukov's promotion to Deputy Supreme Commander, next in rank to Stalin.

The extraordinary kindness of our rediscovered friends overwhelmed us, but did not answer all our needs. Besides, Luba and I felt uncomfortable imposing on them, since they were having difficulty surviving as well. But the small stipend the Institute promised Luba was not sufficient to sustain us. Tashkent had no need for veterinary assistants, and had no other employment opportunities for me.

Hunger pervaded the city, and food grew scarcer. I woke up daily before dawn to join long queues to get our meager portion of bread, but often found that the bakery had run out of all provisions. Zhenya and Mikhail heard rumors that an epidemic

82

of typhoid fever had invaded the city, turning it into a hazard for homeless strangers. The countryside, they agreed with us, would make it easier to find food and a place to live.

I made an appointment to visit the Veterinary Affairs Department of Uzbekistan, which I had located near the city hall. To spruce up, I bought a new shirt for the occasion. I was summoned to see the director of the department, a fluent Russian-speaking Uzbek man in his 40s, much taller than I. He asked me to sit while he reviewed my papers.

In response to his questions about my schooling in Aksai, I enumerated the courses we took, the experience we had on the neighboring farms, and the internship I had just begun before my sister and I had to flee.

"Do you know the Uzbek language?" the director asked. "You know you'll be here among Uzbek people who do not know Russian."

I told him that as children we had to become multilingual, since my birthplace had been overrun by several neighboring nations.

"I see you are a bright young man, and I trust you will apply yourself well to your work." He keyed me in on an opening for an assistant to serve a few farms surrounding Sir Darya, a village about 100 kilometers southwest of Tashkent. Its veterinary services were headed by a man whom he thought I would like to work for, and he offered to write a letter recommending me. He stood up, shook my hand, and bid me goodbye.

I returned to the apartment and elatedly showed Luba the letter. Next day, she went to the Education Department and got a letter of recommendation to the Sir Darya High School principal. In the evening, we told the Kaganoviches of our decision to leave Tashkent.

Next morning, Neena and Mikhail accompanied us to the railroad station.

"Don't forget," Neena said, hugging Luba, "If things don't go well for you in Sir Darya, consider our abode. Wherever we are is your home."

"Yes, you are part of our family," exclaimed Mikhail.

Neena embraced me, as we said goodbye, and I felt tears on her cheeks. The picture of Mother holding me tight on parting a year earlier came to my mind.

Luba and I left, and shortly we boarded a train to Sir Darya.

CHAPTER 6

Living Among Uzbeks –

The Veterinary Assistant

A drizzly day in October 1942 greeted us as we left the train and entered the small, brick railroad station of Sir Darya. A guard directed us to the center of town, a kilometer or so away. The round huts along the dirt road reminded me of the pictures from the *Baba Yaga* stories of my childhood. A plot of land, filled with stalks of corn and other vegetables, enveloped each hut.

In the town hall building, the administrator, sitting at a desk, greeted us in Russian, with a Ukrainian accent. He must have been relocated from Ukraine and sent here, I thought. The letters of recommendation from the state that we presented impressed him. He gave us written notes for our would-be employers: the high school, where Luba was to teach Russian and Russian history, and the veterinary doctor in town. He also suggested we see a woman named Olga, who might have a place to rent.

Olga, an attractive woman in her 50s, blonde with lively, blue eyes, and an easy smile, told us she had arrived in the early 1930s with her husband, a wealthy Ukrainian farmer, who had since died in an accident on the collective farm. She spoke with ease, as she detected our Polish accent, and showed us eagerly a place downstairs, next to her own apartment. She explained that she had another tenant on the upper floor.

The room, about 10-by-12 feet, had an earthen floor, clay walls, and a small stove near the entry. A couch with torn upholstery, on the left, a narrow cot against the opposite wall, a small table, and one chair near the stove completed the furnishings.

She pointed out the outhouse at the end of her property, and a makeshift grill, on top of a few bricks and stones, for outdoor cooking. She showed us how to pump water from the artesian well. She embraced Luba gently and shook my hand before leaving us for a while. Soon she returned with blankets, pillows, another chair, pots and pans, and a couple of plates, as well as food: cabbage soup, potatoes, and half a loaf of bread.

"I hope you will be comfortable here," Olga said.

We unpacked our few belongings and went to sleep.

In the morning, Luba and I went to secure our new jobs. I walked fast, with anticipation, to meet Mahmoud, the veterinarian who lived near the town hall, in a rectangular, wooden-frame structure, which stood in contrast to the mud houses of the other villagers. A woman dressed in a white coat and sitting at a desk in the hallway, greeted me, and asked me, in heavily-accented Russian, to wait. Shortly, Mahmoud warmly welcomed me.

"I received a call from the state veterinary doctor that you would be coming, and I am very happy to see you," he said in fluent Russian, as he firmly shook my hand. I showed him my documents, but he hardly looked at them.

"We're not sticklers on formalities here. I'll try my best to help you do your best," he said, inviting me into his office, a spacious room filled with endless rows of bottles and books.

Mahmoud, in his 40s, with regular Caucasian features—except

for slightly slanted, dark eyes—wore a colorful cylindrical cap and a white coat. Mahmoud made me feel comfortable, and I felt that he took a liking to me.

He asked about my home, my sister, my travels, and my views of the country and Sir Darya. Then he excused himself to see some patients and, before leaving, he handed me a book about animal anatomy. Soon he returned and began to outline the work I would be doing. "First, the people you'd be working with do not understand Russian, and you must learn some Uzbek language to be able to communicate," he said. He reached for a well-worn Uzbek-Russian dictionary, commenting that he had used it a lot through the years. He explained that the Uzbek language words were written in Cyrillic, the Russian alphabet, although the local newspapers used the Arabic alphabet, since the Uzbeks were Muslims and had been imbued with Arab culture before the Russians annexed the country. He suggested that I learn at least a few hundred Uzbek words dealing with basic daily living.

Mahmoud told me about the farms where I would be working: three farms in a semi-circle, about 20 kilometers west of Sir Darya, and mentioned he would get me a horse from the collective farm. He described the work I would be doing to keep the sheep and cattle healthy. The sheep produced tons of wool, essential for survival in the cold climate of most of Russia. The cattle produced meat, particularly important to feed the army, with Ukraine and other meat-producing areas of the Soviet Union now occupied by the Germans.

Eczema presented the most-threatening skin disease to sheep in the area, and while it could not be eliminated entirely, one could control it with special baths. I would have the important task of supervising these mass baths, Mahmoud told me. The farm people would assist me, but it would be my responsibility to see that all sheep got bathed and that none drank the poisonous bath water. He informed me that we would visit a farm where they scheduled a mass bath, and I would see firsthand how this was done. At the same time, we would visit all the farms, so I could meet the chieftains and get acquainted with Uzbek daily living.

In addition to supervising the baths, I would be in charge of castrating hundreds of lambs. Castration, Mahmoud told me, was essential, not only to control the quality of the sheep population, but also to raise healthy males with good, thick fleece. The procedure had to be performed carefully, since a lamb could die from excessive bleeding or infection.

He handed me a book on infectious diseases of cattle, and asked that I study several of the chapters; then, shaking my hand, he left.

I ran back to the cottage, anxious to share my excitement with Luba. I described Mahmoud, and how much I liked him and felt a kinship with him.

"Well, I know you're a genius, but I got a pretty darn good job as well. I'm going to be teaching Russian and Russian literature in the high school," Luba said.

"How would you teach them, not knowing the language?" I asked.

"The high school has a lot of Ukrainian and Russian children, as well as Uzbek children who are required to learn Russian."

She showed me a load of provisions she got from the collective farm.

"Unlike in Aksai, here they treat teachers very well," she said. Excited, she unloaded cabbage, potatoes, corn, and peas, and proceeded to prepare our evening meal, while I immersed myself reading the book Mahmoud had given me.

The rest of the week and the following week, I went daily to

Mahmoud, and he taught me different aspects of taking care of the sheep herds and cattle on the farms. He also gave me beautifully illustrated books on animal anatomy, and a book on castration of animals. The personal attention Mahmoud gave me elated me. The veterinary assistant course I had taken in Aksai now seemed superficial, compared with the material he taught me and the books he made me read.

"How would you like to observe the bathing of sheep at the farms where you'd be working, Meesha?" Mahmoud surprised me one morning.

"That would be great," I said.

"We need to get you a horse first," he said. We went to the nearby collective farm, and the stable keeper selected for me a five-year-old brown horse named Trotter. "He's a good horse, well-trained for long trips," the keeper said, as he fastened the saddle, adjusted the straps, and handed me the reins and whip; he also gave me a bale of hay. "I'll see you 6 a.m. tomorrow morning, Meesha," Mahmoud said, as we parted.

Mounting the horse, I rode to our hut, where I tied him in the adjoining shed, spread out the bale of hay, and brought some water. I went back to our room and resumed my studies.

"Hey, Luba, we are the new owners of a horse!" I exclaimed to Luba when she returned from work. I took her to see the horse, and she shared my excitement.

"So what are you going to do with him?" she asked me, bewildered.

"I'm going to ride the horse from farm to farm, assisting Mahmoud," I answered proudly.

Early next morning, I rode my horse to Mahmoud's place. He greeted me, holding the reins of a beautiful mare, white with black patches, considerably larger than my horse. Dressed in leather breeches and a leather jacket, he mounted his horse, appearing to me as if he were Genghis Khan, confident and spirited, ready to summon his troops.

We traveled through miles of farm land, with long stretches of barren land. The dirt road wound through orchards and small tents interspersed between the tilled fields. Mahmoud pointed at rice paddies filled with water next to canals, and cotton fields in the distance. A few hours later, we reached a farm with a few tents surrounding a common square of land. The round tent walls, made of heavy, dark mats, had conical roofs covered with thatch. We stopped at the largest tent and tied up our horses.

"We're going to see Rahman. I see his horse is here," Mahmoud said, explaining that Rahman was the chieftain of this, the largest farm, as well as the head of the collective farm, which also included the other two farms I would be visiting. Rahman and his assistant, Kasem, were to accompany us to the baths.

Rahman and Kasem soon appeared and exchanged greetings with Mahmoud, who introduced me, as Rahman began haltingly to talk with me in Russian. Rahman, in his 50s, short and stocky, with a round face, a nearly white goatee, well-proportioned nose and mouth, and sharp, green eyes with slightly slanted lids, wore a leather outfit. His gentle smile and soft voice made me feel at ease. Kasem, considerably younger, taller and thinner than Rahman, with dark hair, black moustache, dark eyes, and light complexion, wore working clothes.

The four of us mounted our horses, and trotted off to the outskirts of the farm, where the sheep bathing was to take place. One of the shepherds greeted us and led us to a small cabin containing the bath solutions stored in huge glass vats next to the bath, a 40-by-5-foot clay channel, filled with water. Mahmoud became instantly preoccupied with adding the vat liquids to the baths, as he explained to me how to estimate the required number of vats. Soon a swarm of sheep appeared, coming from the nearby hill. A few shepherds, with the help of dogs, corralled the sheep into the mouth of the channel, consisting of two wooden fences, about a hundred feet apart, and narrowing to line up with the short end of the bath. One by one, the sheep jumped into the bath, and, a few seconds later, emerged at the other end, shaking the water off their bodies and running off into the field. The whole process, however, took several hours to complete.

A beautiful, stately woman greeted us on our return to Rahman's tent, "Salaam, salaam!"

"Salaam to you, my dear Rashmi," Mahmoud answered.

The tent, rich and colorful, had rugs all around, looking like beautiful paintings, with scattered, hand-woven rugs also covering most of the ground. A large, semi-spherical container in a metal tripod stood on top of a hearth, filled with a few simmering coals. One corner of the room held a pile of blankets and pillows, the other contained colorful, bright robes hung on a rope. Near the entrance hung rows of kitchen utensils and pots and pans.

We sat down cross-legged on a rug next to a little round table. A young woman in her teens brought us tea and slices of flat bread. "Meet my daughter, Mahdu," said Rahman, turning to me.

Mahdu bowed her head, and I noticed her blush, as I bowed my head in return.

"Pleasure to meet you," I said in broken Uzbek.

Mahdu, no more than 17—my age—with long dark braids, large black eyes, and soft red lips, wore a beautiful, free-flowing silk dress. She instantly evoked my memories of Sophie. Rahman distracted me: "You like what you see?" he asked.

"Yes," I answered enthusiastically, not knowing quite if he

meant the tent or Mahdu, as we partook of tea and refreshments. Soon Mahmoud turned businesslike, though I could not follow the conversation. Rahman spoke slowly, but with authority, and I sensed that Mahmoud had a lot of respect for him.

An hour later, Mahmoud addressed me quietly. "Rahman invited us to join them for dinner and stay with him and his family for the night. In the morning we'll be off to see the other two farms, and then return to Sir Darya. Now let's feed the horses and wash up."

He led me outside the tent, where Mahdu handed us pitchers of water and small towels. Shortly, we sat down on rugs around the hearth to have dinner, which Rashmi and Mahdu had prepared. We were to share the food from one large, round pot, filled with rice, pieces of lamb, carrots and peppers, but I saw no utensils. Mahmoud noticed that I hesitated. "Use your fingers, just like this," he said, as he reached his hand into the edge of the pot, removed a clump of food, and put it in his mouth. Rahman did the same, and I followed. "This is our favorite food. We call it pilaf," Mahmoud said. I savored the first piece of meat I had eaten in a very long time, and I enjoyed the rice and vegetables soaked with the lamb's fat. Rashmi capped the meal with tea and pastries she had made, dipped in honey.

As evening descended, Rashmi arranged a corner of the tent for us to sleep in, placing a thick, cotton comforter on the rug, with blankets for cover. She then prepared bedding for herself and her family in another part of the tent. A leather-covered, wooden frame partition separated their quarters from ours.

In the morning, Kasem joined us for tea and fruit, and then the three of us mounted our horses again, and we went to see the neighboring farm a few kilometers away. Mahmoud explained to me that a man reporting to Rahman supervised the smaller neighboring farm. Tamir, the head of that farm, had also another farm under his control. That farm, some 10 kilometers away, for which I would be responsible as well, we would not see on this trip, Mahmoud told me.

Tamir waited for us at the first farm, in front of one of the tents, much smaller than Rahman's tent. Mahmoud introduced me to Tamir, who extended his hand to greet me. He had a strong grip, and I felt that he liked me, even though we could not communicate well, with his knowledge of Russian being no better than my command of the Uzbek language. Tamir showed us around his property and invited us to his tent.

The tent, made in a similar fashion to that of Rahman's, had fewer rugs on the circular walls, and only a few scattered on the floor. We sat down on the floor, cross-legged around a small table. Tamir introduced his wife, Leah, who was much younger than Rashmi, maybe in her late 20s. Barefoot, vivacious and full of smiles, she wore a colorful, striped cotton dress. Presently, she brought in a young girl of about five, who sat on Tamir's lap, observing us quietly, while Tamir caressed her hair. Leah returned with tea and pieces of flat bread, slices of cheese, and fresh vegetables. Mahmoud, Kasim, and Tamir started a businesslike conversation, which lasted for some time. Late in the afternoon, Mahmoud and I bid our host goodbye, mounted our horses, and we were off, back to Sir Darya.

On the way, Mahmoud told me that Tamir had another home on the third farm, the one we could not visit on this trip, and that he had another wife in that household. He advised me to be discreet about it when I visited Tamir's second home.

Mahmoud explained that Moslems were allowed to have more than one wife, despite the Soviet government being against it.

"Of course, it's costly to have another home, and women often resent competition. Apparently, Tamir has no difficulty with either problem, and he is a pretty good man, very easy to work with," Mahmoud said.

We arrived in Sir Darya at dusk. I went home and told Luba about my exploits on the farms. Luba's work at school pleased her as well.

"The news from the front is not so good, Mehal," Luba said, when we sat down to eat. "The Germans have tightened their noose around Stalingrad, and street-to-street fighting has spread throughout the city."

I reminded Luba that Norbert had predicted this happening while we were on the train in Kazakhstan. He had worried that if the Germans conquered Stalingrad, they would cut the Russians off from oil; without oil, the Russian fighting machine would come to a halt.

"Don't make it sound like you know everything," Luba said. "Remember, last year Hitler was to enter Moscow and finish off the Soviet Union. It didn't happen, did it?"

I resented Luba putting me down, but I thought she might be right. I remembered how last winter's cold weather paralyzed the German killing machine. Maybe this winter would be no different.

Luba told me she had gone to the military office to inquire about Hershl, telling them how he had disappeared in Voroshilovograd. The man suggested that she write to the headquarters of the Southern army. Luba sent a letter to the address the man had given her. "I've written so many letters, all to no avail," she concluded.

I reminded Luba that the Kaganoviches and the Wieners had not had much luck finding their sons either. Next morning, I went to see Mahmoud.

"You made a good impression, Meesha," he said. "They all seem to like you. You'll get along well with them." He asked if I had read the book on castration he had given me, and reminded me that in the spring we would need to castrate a lot of young lambs.

Meanwhile, he wanted me to spend much time on the farms, since he had promised Rahman that I would be assigned to the three farms full-time. He wanted me to visit each farm at least once a week, and urged me to be alert and report to him any illnesses or problems I detected.

Two days later, I started out on my own to see Rahman, who was waiting for me when I arrived. After a quick breakfast, he handed me over to Kasem, who mounted his horse and took me around to see the herds in the adjoining pastures. He introduced me to the shepherds, and then took me to see the horses and the cattle grazing on the farm. Late in the afternoon, we went to Tamir's farm, which we had not been able to see on our visit with Mahmoud, and I met his second wife.

Sarrat, in her 40s, was quite a bit shorter than Leah, Tamir's other wife. She walked with a cane, limping on her right foot. Her small, round face projected a friendly, kind smile. She looked straight at me, and her dark eyes appeared sad; I instantly understood why. Tamir spoke to her harshly, and though I did not understand much, I sensed he was not happy with her. Shortly two teenage boys came in.

"These are my two sons, Ishmael and Ibrahim. They are big boys now and are a great help to me," Tamir said.

Tamir took me inside the hut. We sat down, cross-legged, around a large, deep metal pot, as we had in Rahman's tent a few days earlier. The pot, filled with pilaf, had far fewer pieces of meat mixed with the rice. Kasem and Tamir left, and I stayed in the tent with Sarrat and the two boys. Sarrat unrolled a heavy mat, gave me a pillow and a blanket, and showed me where I could sleep for the night. In the morning, she gave me flat bread with cheese and tea, and soon I went off to see the herd.

Late November 1942 brought balmy weather, with the sun shining brightly, in contrast to the rainy October. I felt exhilarated as I headed home to see Luba after days of work. I dismounted Trotter, and I picked a couple of melons left in the field along the road, putting them in the two-sided sack stretched across the horse's back.

I came home and spent a peaceful weekend with Luba, the first weekend in which I felt we were out of danger. Luba had a few books that she had taken out of the school library, and we shared the delights of Turgenev, Gorky, and Gogol, as we read by candlelight until the wee hours of the morning.

In the weeks that followed, I repeated my trips to the farms nearly every week, also spending some time with Mahmoud. I liked the work, but the excitement of the first few weeks began to wear off. All-day trips on horseback became more tiring; most of all, they grew lonesome.

A vision of Uncle Hershl Ackerman appeared to me on my return to Sir Darya one day. I saw him as on the day he blessed me, after visiting us a few years earlier. Tall and stately, he carried himself like an aristocrat, and he spoke like one, too, quietly, with authority, weighing each word with care, as if it were on trial.

People addressed him reverently *Der Rov*, as the rabbi of Targowicze, my father's hometown, some 20 miles from Dubno, where we had lived. Mother called him *Der Dayan*, the Judge, for in addition to being the titular head of the Jewish community of Targowicze, he served as a judge of considerable renown. He had traveled throughout the region and participated in, often presided over, trials – known as *Din-Torahs* – between Jews, involving civil and business disputes.

The trials had brought Uncle Hershl many times to my town and home, where he would stay for the duration of the proceedings. I had cherished those occasions, since he would share the very room where my sister and I slept. We lived in a two-room house, with an attached kitchenette, and the front room facing the street served as the living room, guest room, and the room where my older sister and I did our homework and slept. Mother would convert the brown, leather couch on the wall opposite our beds into a sleeping abode for my great-uncle.

In the fall of 1936, Uncle Hershl visited us for the last time. He came into my room late in the evening, after long discussions with my parents. I was busy drawing a picture by the faint light of a kerosene lamp.

"You're not asleep yet, Mehal?" he asked quietly, so as not to awaken my sister, motioning me to sit next to him on the couch. "What are you drawing?" he asked.

"It's a picture of the poet Bialik," I said, showing him the face I had drawn, with one eye smudged from repeated erasures.

"Try to move on to new things," he said. "Don't go back, move on, move on, Mehal."

Next morning, Father asked me to accompany Uncle Hershl to the bus station for his trip home. We walked through a small park, with Uncle holding my hand. As we approached the station, Uncle turned towards me, grabbed my face in his palms and recited the traditional blessing of the *Kohanim*, the priests of Israel. "May God bless you and keep you! .... May He lift His face unto you and give you peace!" He lifted me gently and kissed me on the cheeks, his warm tears wetting my face. He put me down and stepped into the bus.

Autumn gave way to a cold winter. Uncle braved the elements,

Dayan Hershl Axelrod, author's great-uncle.

and left to preside over a trial in Luczk, about 30 kilometers from his home. A few days after his arrival, he unexpectedly passed away, on Friday afternoon. Upon learning of his death, a hundred or so men of Targowicze left on the Sabbath, on foot, and early next day carried his body back for burial. Uncle's blessing haunted me. Was it a blessing to be amidst strangers in a strange land? Worry about the fate of my parents and all my relatives and friends began to crowd my mind. Would I ever see my hometown again? Would Luba and I be stuck here forever? Was Hitler going to prevail, after all? These thoughts became more persistent and disturbing on my long rides.

In late November, the war bulletins in the newspapers Luba brought from the library became more hopeful. Fierce fighting continued near Stalingrad, and in the northern region of the Caucus, and in areas between the Don and the Volga Rivers. On November 20, the newspaper reported a routing of the Romanian forces in a Soviet breakthrough, southwest of Stalingrad. A few days later, a war bulletin announced the capture of 30,000 Romanian soldiers, including many high-ranking officers and generals.

In December, the weather turned unpleasant, raining almost daily, and the nights changing to freezing cold. The roads became muddy, making them more difficult for Trotter to negotiate. I often came to Sarrat's tent wet and shivering from the cold. She treated me as if I were her older son, giving me hot tea, and hanging up my wet denim jacket to dry next to the hearth in the middle of the tent.

Unpleasant episodes began to mar my relations with Sarrat. One morning after I had come in chilled the evening before, the blanket and bedding Sarrat had prepared for me were all wet when I awoke. I did not know enough of the Uzbek language to express my regrets to Sarrat, but she saw my embarrassment. A kind woman, she stretched out the bedding to make sure it would dry for the night, but the next night, the wetting episode happened again.

On my return to Sir Darya, I went to see a doctor in the hospital. He suspected that the incidents resulted from tension and stress. The wetting accidents kept repeating for quite awhile: I understood the doctor, but my body did not. Worse than that, I had terrible nightmares, seeing Father in a pool of blood, and Mother's pale head next to him. I moved close to them, and almost touched them, then woke up shivering, in a cold sweat. I took a week off on the advice of the doctor, stayed in the hut, read books, and daydreamed of my home, parents, Sophie, and years of study at the private Hebrew school in Ostrog. At the end of the week, I felt stronger and resumed my work on the farms.

Towards the end of January 1943, great news of the German surrender near Stalingrad flooded the airwaves and the press. More than 300,000 German soldiers, a whole army led by Field Marshal Paulus, had surrendered. Detailed newspaper accounts described the brilliant Soviet Army strategies that had led to the victory. In the late fall of 1942, the Soviets had built enormous reserves of men and material, under artful camouflage, on the eastern shores of the Volga River. In December, those reserves poured stealthily across the frozen Volga River, catching the German armies unaware. The Red Army, under Zhukov, proceeded to surround the German armies in and around Stalingrad, and in early January completed the encirclement of the main German forces. Subsequent aircraft and artillery bombardment of the trapped German army forced their surrender.

The Germans' push to conquer Stalingrad had ended. Suddenly the Soviet army was on the march, pushing the German army westward.

The news from the front and the balmy weather rejuvenated my spirit in the spring of 1943. My Uzbek language began to improve, and I could talk with the people on the farms. Sarrat's complaints and suffering about her competitor, the younger wife of Tamir, particularly touched me, as I began to feel a kinship with her. "The whore did it again," she complained one day, pointing to the small piece of lamb Tamir had left her. "As usual, she has stolen most of the meat and left this pittance for me and my boys." Sarrat's sorry state and her bitterness reminded me of Mahmoud's comments he had made earlier about the difficulties of being married to more than one wife.

"How did you like the book on castration of animals I gave you?" Mahmoud asked me, when I visited him after a long absence.

"I loved it; I found it fascinating!" I answered.

Mahmoud told me that a woman in the waiting room wanted him to castrate her lamb, and that he would like me to assist him. He grabbed his instruments and arranged them on the table where he would do the operation. He went to the waiting room and came back with a white lamb, a few months old. He directed me to hold the lamb very carefully and strongly as he went to wash his hands.

He came back with a small basin of warm water, a packet of cotton, a scalpel, a bottle of iodine, a few other medicinal bottles, and containers of powder. He washed and anesthetized the scrotum, made the one-inch incision, pulled out the testicles one at a time, cut the ligaments and the blood vessels away from the testicles, sprinkled some iodine and disinfectant powder on the wound, and stitched the scrotum.

The lamb bleated plaintively, and Mahmoud lifted it in his

arms. Mahmoud's skills impressed me: the procedure took barely 10 minutes and caused very little bleeding.

"So, now you know all about castration," he said. "In a few days, we'll be doing a lot of these on the farm."

"That will be great!" I said.

I returned to the farms to supervise the bathing of the sheep. Within a space of two weeks, I organized baths at all three farms, for thousands of sheep. Mahmoud came out to observe the first bath, but left a few hours later, patting me on the back. "You're doing just fine!" he said.

A week or two later, we scheduled a castration at the smaller farm. Mahmoud came out for the first day and went over the main procedure again. He castrated the first couple of lambs, and then watched me do it for an hour or two; and being satisfied, he left me in charge. I felt thrilled at how quickly I learned to do the procedure, without much bleeding or any other mishaps. Seeing the bleating lambs running off to the pastures, as if nothing had happened, pleased me to no end; learning a few weeks later that all the castrated lambs had healed well filled me with pride. I gained much respect from the shepherds and with Rahman, Tamir, and Kasem, and they started calling me Dr. Bolassi (the boy doctor).

At the end of March, when I came home to visit Luba, she told me excitedly that the school had arranged for all teachers to get plots of land for their use. She had spoken to Sergey, the tenant who lived upstairs in Olga's cottage, and he had advised that we should plant mosh, the small peas we had been eating. He claimed that in the past few years, the farm had excellent crops of mosh, and he expected this year to be no different. Later in the afternoon, we went to see Sergey upstairs, and he accompanied us to the farm.

Sergey, in his late 50s or early 60s, short and stocky, had a round face, lively blue eyes full of fun, and red hair wildly scattered over his nearly bald head. A former assistant chieftain of the farm, now mostly retired, he had lots of friends on the farm and in the village. He lived alone, having been separated from his family when he had been picked up by Stalin's police from his large farm in Ukraine in the mid-30s and sent here. Easy to converse with, he took a liking to Luba.

Luba and I spent long hours reading books she took out of the school library. We were also delighted to hear the young people of the village singing Russian and Ukrainian songs late into the night. They had beautiful resonant voices, and would harmonize as if led by a choir master.

In August 1943, *Pravda* reported a great Soviet victory in the Kursk and Smolensk region, where Zhukov's forces encircled and inflicted enormous losses on the German army, essentially eliminating the German forces in the central theater of war. It reinforced mounting optimism that the Soviet Union had turned its fortunes around, on its way to winning the war.

Fall harvest time brought great news to Luba and me: our little plot of land yielded enormous amounts of mosh, which the farm was going to thrash, put in bags, and deliver to us; furthermore, they would reseed the plot for the winter crop. Suddenly, unexpectedly, we felt secure, with plenty of food to eat and some of it to sell. What a difference from the starvation conditions in Aksai the year before!

One morning in early September, I awoke hot and perspiring. I had planned to visit the farms, but I could hardly get out of bed. Luba went to the hospital and learned that I must have contracted typhoid fever, for the illness was spreading through the area. The doctors, knowing of no cure, suggested I take aspirin and have bed rest. A few days later, feeling much better, I planned to resume my farm visits. However, the next morning, Luba complained about the same symptoms, but her fever soon shot up to the point where she became delirious. Sergey helped me to get a horse and wagon from the farm, and we took Luba to the hospital. I stayed with her until a kind doctor assured me that Luba would be all right.

I had to visit the farms, and when I returned three days later, Luba's fever had shot up again. This time, the doctor, concerned, advised me to stay close by for the next few days. I stayed with my horse in the adjoining little park, where I slept on one of the benches for the next two nights. I was frightened that Luba might die.

When Sergey and I came to fetch her with a horse and wagon, I could hardly recognize her: she looked like a skeleton, with her braids all gone, and her eyes sunken and motionless.

"You're a good brother," the doctor said. "You'll need to continue being good to her. The illness has affected her mind, as typhoid fever does sometimes. I hope she'll pull out of that difficulty, but she'll need a lot of loving care."

We took Luba home and put her gently to bed. I fetched a chicken from the farm and prepared a meal Mother used to make—chicken soup with potatoes, carrots, and other vegetables. Then I grilled a piece of chicken, put it on a platter, and helped Luba sit up, but she would not eat. I prompted her gently, but to no avail. Furthermore, she would not speak to me; she seemed unable to utter a word. I mounted my horse; panic-stricken, I returned to the hospital. "What should I do, doctor, what should I do?" I asked the doctor.

"I'm afraid there's nothing you can do. You have to give it time, patience, and love," she replied.

"What are the chances my sister will get well?" I persisted.

"Fifty-fifty," she replied.

I came back and Luba motioned she wanted to drink. That gave me an idea. I cooked the chicken in the soup until the meat was very soft. I tore the chicken into small pieces and mashed the contents of the pot with a fork, until they became almost liquid. I poured some of the liquid into a glass, and fed it slowly to Luba. She liked it, and this became her diet, in small quantities.

Slowly, she began to eat some soft vegetables, and then pieces of meat. But she remained speechless and unresponsive. I cajoled her, begged her to talk to me, told her funny stories, and reminded her of us playing as children at home; she listened with vacant eyes, staring in the distance, without uttering a word.

"Luba, Lubushka, wake up!" I pleaded with her in utter frustration. I bathed her with water warmed on the grill, and tended to all her needs. I felt a deep, overwhelming love for her, mixed with worry, concern, and despair. In the night's quietude, I recited psalms that I remembered, and spoke to my parents, begging for their help.

Two weeks went by. Mahmoud assigned another young man to visit the farms. I began to doubt Luba would ever get well. The thought of losing Luba petrified me. Our relationship during the past few years had become symbiotic. I felt I could not live without her, without her will to live and to fight, without her ingenuity to survive amidst the chaos of the war.

I remembered Father's charge, "Take good care of Luba." Have I? I wondered.

One morning, nearly a month after Luba had fallen ill, I woke up reflecting about my home. It was the time of the year when we celebrated *Rosh Hashona,* the Jewish New Year. I remembered Mother, Father, Luba, and me sitting around the festive table and

Father praising the way I chanted my solo at the Great Synagogue, *Haben Yakeer Lee Ephrayin* (I will remember my dear son, Ephrayin, said the Lord). I began humming the tune. Then, seeing Luba stir, I sang louder, enunciating clearly each word, and chanting each note with all the care and beauty I could muster. Suddenly, Luba started singing along with me, tentatively at first, then more confidently as we went on.

"Luba, Lubushka, you sing so beautifully!" I embraced her and covered her face with gentle kisses. "You'll be all right now!" I exclaimed, with tears in my eyes.

"Thank you, Mehal," Luba said.

Slowly, she began to recover. In a few days, Luba was back on her feet, and a week later, she returned to work.

Feverish activity filled my next two months. Mahmoud put me in charge of conducting the baths, as well as taking care of all veterinary matters on the farms. Staying through that period on the farms, I began to feel comfortable and at ease; the women of the three farms adopted me, as if I were a part of their families. Rahman's daughter, Mahdu became especially friendly. One evening, as I arrived and tied up my horse near Rahman's tent, she came out with a pitcher of water to wash my hands. Then she gently caressed me and whispered, "I like you, I like you very much." A warm sweetness raced through my body.

"You're beautiful," I whispered, gently caressing her dark, flowing hair. We entered the tent as if nothing had happened. But, she stirred my feelings, filling me with excitement and turmoil. I could not blot out her face, her full lips, and dark eyes burning with desire; I could not drive out of my mind, the softness of her hair, and the sweetness of her caress.

I found her mysteriously beautiful and attractive; it also dawned on me that her parents had begun to treat me as their

106

potential son-in-law. Yet I feared becoming trapped, away from my people and my faith. Would I ever see my people again? A torrent of conflicts began to tear me apart. I felt shaken: I was neither a Jew nor an Uzbek, alone, without roots, without a home.

"We want you to sign these documents." Rahman turned to me one evening, after a gathering of the chieftains in his tent. Rahman explained that the documents dealt with the disappearance of ten sheep. He wanted me to confirm that the sheep had died because of an infection. My ears perked up. I told him this would cause a lot of questions, since I was supposed to report all infectious diseases to Mahmoud.

"Don't worry about it," Rahman said. "We have taken care of Mahmoud, and you have permission from him to sign the papers." I hesitated, apprehensively.

"Look," he went on, "We're all one large family, and we help each other, and we treat you like family, don't we? You sleep here, you eat with us, we do you favors, and we expect you to return the favors."

I signed the papers. Two weeks later, in mid-October 1943, a few inspectors came from Tashkent headquarters to survey the farms and review documents. Sure enough, they found the documents I had signed, and asked me for explanations. I told them the truth, and I became unsettled and worried. Would this be another fiasco like the one in Aksai? I went back to Sir Darya and saw Mahmoud. He had already learned about the fraud.

"I asked you so many times to report to me any irregularities, as well as diseases of the herd. You should have checked with me before signing these papers!" he shouted angrily. "If you get involved in anything like that again, I'll have to fire you."

I apologized profusely and left. On my way to our hut, I pondered about the gravity of what I had done. I felt ashamed and guilty that I had disappointed Mahmoud, a good man and a real friend. I became angry at what the chieftains had forced me to do. They knew very well they had committed a fraud and decided to use me as a scapegoat. They had lied to me. I felt the need to be very careful with the chieftains and their families. I also felt ashamed that I had responded to Mahdu's advances. Don't you ever dare to touch her, I admonished myself.

Christmas 1943 brought news of German retreat and of Soviet forces scoring victories, liberating more than half the Soviet territory that the Germans had occupied. New reserves reinforced the Soviet army. New factories in the liberated areas swelled production capabilities of military aircraft and equipment, which kept rolling out to the front, increasing Soviet superiority in the air and on the ground. Good news also came of Allied Forces' victories in el Alamein in North Africa, and of the Allies' landing in Italy.

Life in the village became more comfortable and vodka more easily available. One afternoon, returning from the farms, I found our hut empty; Luba must have gone to see Olga, I thought. Presently, Sergey came in, waddling like a duck, and sat down on my bed. His eyes were bloodshot, his face all flushed, his mouth covered with froth, and he breathed heavily.

"The son of a bitch—the Georgian murderer!" he shouted. "Where's my wife now? Where are my Ivan and Ludmeela? Where's my home and everything I worked for all my life?" He began sobbing. In a while, he resumed his monologue, more loudly and angrily than before. "They talk as if they love people and want to do good, but they're all bastards. You hear me? They're all horrible bastards; they're killers—Stalin and all his gang. They've killed millions of good people and scattered the rest of us all over Siberia and this Godforsaken place. You know, they tell you they're fighting Hitler because Hitler is a bad man. Stalin is no better! Oh no! He taught Hitler how to take innocent people and send them to slave labor camps where they would freeze to death! And what did they do to me and my family? Where is my love, my wonderful woman? Where are my children?" He began sobbing again.

I became petrified, fearing that someone might hear Sergey's harangue and report us to the NKVD. Sergey's rantings against Stalin were a capital offense, punishable by a death squad, or at the least, spending the rest of one's life in a slave labor camp in Siberia. I took off Sergey's boots and helped him to stretch out on my bed. Soon he collapsed into a deep sleep. Luba returned towards dusk, with some food that Olga had given her. While we ate our meal, I told the surprised Luba, in a hushed voice, what had happened. A few hours later, Sergey woke up and embraced me and then went upstairs.

On the eve of the new year of 1944, Olga invited Luba, together with her friends, some of whom were Uzbek, to a small party. I stayed in our room while Luba went to Olga's spacious kitchen, filled with a dozen or so women and an Uzbek soldier, a boyfriend of one of the women. I could hear laughter and singing, and nearly fell asleep. Suddenly, I heard shouting and commotion. I ran out and opened the kitchen door. The Uzbek soldier was holding Luba, who was shouting, "Let me go! Let me go!" The women crowded around the soldier and began shouting and pushing him.

I stepped forward and lunged at the soldier. The soldier turned to me with rage, shouting, "Get out of here, you little dirty Jew, or I'll kill you!" I tried to punch him, but he avoided me, and pulled out a knife from his back pocket. The women started screaming. Then Sergey appeared out of nowhere. "Drop the knife, or I'll kill you!" he yelled at the soldier, punching him in the face. The soldier staggered and dropped the knife.

"Get the hell out of here." Sergey shouted, and the soldier obliged. I grabbed Sergey's hand and thanked him, and accompanied Luba to our room.

"Everything seemed to be nice. Then he got drunk and attacked me. You saw the rest of it," Luba said, shaking from fright.

I became frightened too, at the thought that Luba might have been raped. I was also enraged by this soldier, returning from the front, with the notion of "dirty Jew." So Hitler's poisons were penetrating, even to this far corner of the Soviet Union.

CHAPTER 7

Serving Briefly in the Army –

The Soloist

I n early January 1944, on my way home from the farms, the day turned raw and windy. Dark, heavy clouds moved in, threatening to burst and engulf the town. Chilly, tired, and hungry, I anxiously anticipated seeing Luba.

Trotter knew we were getting close to home and quickened his pace. We moved along the narrow, winding, nearly frozen, dirt roads. Round, white huts with thatched roofs, like overgrown mushrooms, lined both sides of the road. The small plots of land on the sides, the rear, or in front of each hut looked denuded, with remnants of barren stalks of corn or occasional scarecrows standing like skeletons, evoking memories of summer, when lush vegetation covered each plot.

As we approached our little hut, I spurred the horse into a trot. Soon I spotted Luba lighting a fire on the outside grill. I stopped the horse abruptly near her. "Hi! Lubushka, Galubushka," I exclaimed jovially, using the first words of a popular Russian song Luba was fond of. She turned around, startled. Her face pale and drawn, her lips tight, and her eyes half-open with fear, she looked as if she were holding back her tears.

"Anything the matter?" I asked with concern.

"Tie up your horse and hurry. I have a surprise for you," she said curtly. She is so vulnerable, I thought; she has not yet fully recovered from her bout with typhoid fever. She had lost a lot of her strength, vitality, and determination. Her hair, her beautiful hair, had hardly grown back, and she reminded me of someone who had just returned from prison.

I tied Trotter at the shed near the hut, took off the saddle, and hung it up. I gave him a pail of water and a bale of hay. I then took off the double bag with a melon in each pocket that hung across his torso, a gift from Sarrat, and went inside.

I unloaded the melons and sat across from my sister at the little table.

"So what's the matter, Luba?" I asked.

"Here, read it," she answered, as she flung a letter at me.

I opened the letter, a notice from the military draft people that I was to report for duty the very next morning.

"They're really in a hurry, aren't they?" I said.

"I got the letter a couple of days ago, but didn't know how to reach you. Anyway, you're not going," she stated.

"What do you mean?" I asked. "What do you want me to do?"

"You told me Mahmoud would give you special papers to exempt you as his essential helper in a critical occupation. Why don't you go tomorrow to see him and get the papers from him?"

I told Luba that Mahmoud was away for two weeks in Tashkent, attending a conference of Uzbek veterinarians. He had been put in charge of the veterinary services for the whole region around Samarkand.

"Why don't you wait out the two weeks? Go to one of the farms for some time and wait till Mahmoud gets back. Then you'll see him and go to the military draft people to ask for the exemption," Luba persisted.

112

I explained that Mahmoud's promise to exempt me from the army was just an off-the-cuff remark, and it was made several months ago. Meanwhile, the army has suffered terrible casualties. "As you hear and read in the news, they desperately need more people," I said, "so, even if Mahmoud gives me the letter, it may be of no use at this point."

"But you're wrong, wrong, wrong! Why can't you wait a few weeks? What do you have to lose?" she screamed.

"Luba, you make it sound as if I'm being taken for execution. I want to go to the army to help fight Hitler. The news of mass graves, probably of Jews, makes me mad. Isn't it time that I kill a few Germans?"

"You're not a killer! You don't know how to kill," she said heatedly. "You have to know how to hate before you can kill, and you don't know that either."

"Luba, this country hasn't been so bad to us. We've been able to survive here, while the Jews from Poland and the rest of Europe are being slaughtered. I'm healthy, strong, and I have a responsibility to fight alongside other young people."

"Mehal, you're healthy, but you're not very strong! And you're not a fighter. You don't know how to fight."

"But Luba, you agree that I'm pretty decent and fair. I have to be able to live in peace with myself for the rest of my life. Will you or others respect me if I shirk my duty and go AWOL?"

"Your most important duty is to stay alive. You may be the only male survivor on Father's side, as well as on Mother's side. No civilized nation has the right to take a sole survivor of a whole family to the army to fight in a war. Furthermore, you're from Poland. You're not a Soviet citizen. They have no right to take you to the army in the first place."

"So what do you want me to do? Write a letter to Stalin?"

"Do you remember what our parents said to us? Mother asked me to take care of you, and Father wanted you to take care of me. Is this how you're going to take care of me, leaving me here in the wilderness?" Luba reproached me.

"Luba, we've been together for nearly two-and-a-half years. We shared whatever bread we had, and sometimes I would cheat to favor you when dividing the bread. When you became ill, I was there for you day and night. I tried to protect you as best as I could, and when that monster Uzbek tried to attack you, I nearly lost my life doing so. But I cannot dodge my responsibilities. I don't think Mother and Father would want me to, either."

"When I was near death in the hospital with typhoid, I fought back because of you. If you're gone, I have no reason to want to live. Do you understand?!" She burst out crying. I hugged her, trying to console her. Slowly, Luba's arguments began to sink into my mind. Leaving her alone, barely two months since her serious illness, appeared heartless to me. Maybe she was right, I thought. Finally, we agreed that I would plead with draft authorities the next day, asking them to rescind their order because of my Polish citizenship. At the very least, I would ask them for two weeks' delay, so that the chief veterinarian could prepare proper papers for my exemption. Luba quieted down, and we made peace.

Luba ran out to revive the fire in the grill and warmed up a dish of small peas from the full sack we had in the corner, next to the stove. She unwrapped our daily ration of bread and we ate.

As she was cleaning up, I asked her how she would survive if I was drafted.

"I thought we agreed you wouldn't go to the army!" Luba shouted angrily. "So why are you asking this question?"

"Suppose that they take me, regardless of my arguments. What are you going to do?" I asked.

"I'll manage. Don't worry about me. I did save some money, and the collective farm owes us much more grain they're keeping in store for us from last fall's crop. Thank goodness you took care of the little plot of land I got from the collective farm. And, of course, I'll continue teaching, or maybe I'll go to Samarkand, where there must be Jews from Poland."

I got up and collected the few belongings I would take with me, in case I was drafted, as we retired. Luba lay down in the bed on the outside wall of the room and soon went to sleep. I stretched out on the cot against the adjoining wall. Instantly, waves of doubt and fear began to flood my mind and send shivers through my body. Luba was so often right. She was so much more mature and street smart. What if the draft people did not listen to my pleas, and I had to leave Luba alone? This was no place for a single young Jewish woman. The New Year's Eve incident with the Uzbek assaulting Luba was still fresh in my mind. I feared that this place would become more dangerous yet, as more soldiers returned from the front, infected with the anti-Semitic virus.

Another thought came to me. Luba was right that I did not know how to fight. I remembered being beaten up in public school time and again, and I would never fight back. Always the smallest in class, and not very strong, I felt helpless. I would come home and complain to Mother. Luba would often tease me, "Mother's boy."

Yet another idea startled me. The home upbringing and the Hebrew school education imbued us Jewish children with a culture that abhorred violence and urged us to avoid fights. Ironically, the Christians preached "turn the other cheek," but the Jews actually practiced it; the Christians learned to fight. I began to doubt my ability to be a fighter and felt weak and fearful. It must have been long past midnight before I fell asleep.

In the morning, the fresh air promised a sunny day. Luba and I had tea and the remaining morsels of bread. A cold wintry wind startled me as I tended to my horse. I went inside to fetch my bundle of personal belongings, and Luba and I went off to the military draft station. We joined a line of young people and their accompanying families, filling the little office next to town hall.

"Remember, Mehal, tell them you're a Polish citizen, and that the draft order was mistakenly sent to you. Tell them you're essential in your work as a veterinarian. Don't forget, Mehal," Luba said.

Soon my turn did come, and I confronted a short, stocky man of about 40, with blond hair and penetrating blue eyes. "Your papers, *tovarishch.*"

I took out all my papers and put them before him, including the ones showing I had graduated from the veterinary school.

"I don't need the ones from the veterinary school," he said, and pushed the papers back at me.

"I'm a veterinarian doing essential work here," I said.

"You'll be practicing your trade when you get back. Now let's go through your registration quickly."

"But, I'm also a Polish citizen, and I should be exempt from service," I continued, hesitantly.

"You'll take up that question when you get to your unit. I am here to register you, and that's all."

I let Luba down, I thought, as I mumbled an angry goodbye to the officer. I went back to the other room where I left Luba. "Luba, the guy wouldn't even listen to me; I lost my case and I'll have to leave you now. "

She did not utter a word; she embraced me and began sobbing. A few minutes later, she quieted down and collected her thoughts. "What should I do with the horse, Mehal?"

"Take it to the collective farm, and they'll deliver it to Mahmoud. Say goodbye to Sergey; he has been good to me, and I hope he'll be helpful to you, too. Don't forget to check on the grain the collective farm owes us, and take good care of yourself."

"Mehal, please write, as often as you can."

"Are you going to stay here, Luba?"

"I'm not sure. If we lose contact, use our Dubno home address as a last resort. I will try to get back home as soon as the war ends. Mehal, be very careful. You may be the only one I have left in this world." She was near tears again when she turned around and left.

I stepped back inside a large room where we were told to undress, and I went through a physical exam. Soon a woman orderly served us bread, beans, and cold borsht. Around noon, two dozen of us were taken by horse and wagon to the railroad station. I boarded one of the cars of the train waiting at the station and sat near a window. Our journey took us through open fields, endless and barren, crossed by canals and dams, with some of the plots filled with water for rice farming. Now and then, we passed small collective farms with large, circular tents, the living abodes of the Uzbek farmers. Large herds of sheep appeared, grazing in the hills. Far in the distance, faintly visible, rose the snow-capped foothills of the Himalayas.

An officer in his late 20s or early 30s, wearing well-polished boots, a long, gray coat with red epaulets, and an officer's hat with a red band all around, entered the car.

"Comrades," he began with a big smile, "we're going to a very fine military training place, not far from Kattaqurghan. You'll spend a few months there learning the art and science of war. We want you to become good soldiers. It is young people like you, skilled to fight, who'll help us defeat the monstrous enemy." He went on, quoting from Lenin and Stalin and ending with a boisterous, "Long live the Soviet Union! Long live our great leader, Yosif Vissaryonovich Stalin!" and then he was gone.

My mind wandered, recovering from the shock of the morning and the evening before. The unthinkable was happening. Luba and I had been separated! What was Luba going to do? I owed her so much, I owed her my life, and I was abandoning her! She had an uncanny way of sensing and confronting perils, saving us so many times from possible death. She grew taller and taller in my mind, as my protector, as if she were my mother!

But a curious thought took hold of me: Having a mother made me feel secure, but it also made me feel dependent, relying on somebody else. Mother had loved me and had been protective of me, and Luba extended that relationship. Something within me had begun to rebel long before this call to army duty. I had to stand on my own feet; I had to grow up and face the world on my own. That was the real reason I had ignored Luba's advice to hide for a few weeks and wait until Mahmoud returned to Sir Darya to get me an exemption from the army.

"What have you got to lose?" Luba had kept repeating in despair the evening before, but I never answered that question. Yes, I would have a chance to be on my own now, but I wondered, at what price?

The train came to a halt. Several trucks at the station took us a few kilometers to a military base on the outskirts of Kattaqurghan. We disembarked and entered a long barrack. We had to register and get our wardrobe, military gear, and canteen. Assigned to a group of about 15 other young inductees, I started a new life as a Soviet soldier.

A young man in his 20s with a pleasant smile and voice introduced himself. "I am Andrey Petrovich Sokolov. I am your sergeant, and I will be in charge of training you to become good soldiers."

We introduced ourselves and gave a brief summary of our background. I explained that I had been born in Poland, had run away with my sister from the advancing German armies, and had landed in Uzbekistan. Andrey showed us to our bunks, instructed us on how to make our beds, how to take care of our rifles, and told us about our daily routine. He also showed us how to wrap our legs with heavy, cotton ribbons to protect our legs from injury.

At dinnertime, we went to the mess hall, where we were served cabbage soup with potatoes and quite a bit of meat. An hour or so of indoctrination on Communist ideology, with particular emphasis on Stalin's book, *Questions of Leninism,* followed dinner. We went to our bunks, conscious of the need to rise at 6 a.m.

The next two days we spent inside the compound, listening to introductions of the various units, services, functions and responsibilities of each, the nature of our training program, and political lectures. On the third day, we ventured out of the compound in military gear to faraway plains where the military exercises took place. The march was accompanied with song, started by a zapyevala (soloist), and followed by the others in the refrain. Andrey picked the tallest guy in the first column of the first row to be the soloist. He had a loud voice, but sang off-key. Being the shortest among the 16 men in the group, I marched in the last row. I joined in the refrain and, hesitating at first, I tried to bring the music back to a steady key, using my musical training as a soloist in the Great Synagogue of Dubno before the war. This caught Andrey's attention, and on the way back from the exercises, he turned to me and said, "You start a song!" I began singing *Katyusha*, a popular Russian song. I sang well, and felt thrilled when everyone joined enthusiastically in the refrain.

As we got to the barracks, everybody praised me and patted me on the back and pronounced, "Maladyetz, maladyetz (great job, great job)." Being a soloist in the army was, apparently, a great honor. The Russians loved to sing, as I had learned from my years on the various collective farms. The soloist played an important role, enlivening the troops, helping them cope with exhaustion or with the challenge of combat. Later in the evening, I learned that the role also had a downside.

After dinner, I left the mess hall in the dark, heading towards the barracks, when Ivan, the former soloist, suddenly appeared in front of me.

"Why did you take the job away from me?" he yelled, with a voice full of anger.

"I didn't do any such thing. Andrey asked me to start singing."

"You're lying, you dirty little Jew," he continued furiously.

"No, I am not lying and don't call me a dirty Jew," I countered.

"Why, you want to fight me? You wouldn't anyway because you are a coward."

Suddenly he swung with all force at my jaw, as I tried vainly to protect myself. When I finally opened my eyes, after being knocked unconscious, Ivan had gone. During the introductions, he had mentioned that he had been born in Ukraine. I knew from my earlier experiences in Poland that Ukrainians hated Jews. "Anti-Semitism has no borders," I remembered Mr. Wiener saying, on our flight from Stalingrad.

I felt bitter, helpless and lonely. Then I remembered another bloody encounter I had had in public school several years earlier.

"Yanek beat me up again," I complained to Mother, holding back my tears, while pressing a handkerchief against my bloody nose.

Mother caressed me and then said softly, "He is jealous of you, Mehal, you understand? You're a very good pupil and you tend to show off; that makes other kids jealous. Be careful, Mehal."

120

I kept writing letters to Luba, almost daily. I told her about my exciting promotion to be the soloist of our small platoon. I wrote to her about our exercises in the fields, and how good it felt to be part of the huge defense enterprise. I wanted to cheer her up, make sure she would not worry about me. I waited anxiously to hear from her, but I did not get any reply. In fact, none of the other soldiers in the group received any letters either, and that worried me.

Weeks went by in basic training. We would march out of the compound and walk sometimes as far as six or seven kilometers to reach the training fields. There we would engage in running, climbing over hurdles and obstacles, lifting ourselves by holding onto ropes, and learning how to crawl with our heads down, often in mud. Exhausted, we would march back to the compound. I lost a lot of weight, though I felt quite healthy, at least for a while.

Time went by, and my worries increased, as I did not get a single letter from my sister. In fact, I did not even get an answer to my letters to Mahmoud, although I dismissed that, thinking that Mahmoud must have been busy trying to replace me. But I felt certain that Luba would answer my letters immediately. I inquired at the main office repeatedly, and the officer assured me that my letters had gone out and I should not worry.

The horrible dreams of earlier, harder times revisited me. I saw my father lying in a pool of blood with his throat cut open, screaming for help. Mother was next to him, but I saw only her head, with her dark hair arranged neatly in a bun, her face pale, almost white, and her brown eyes motionless. Her tight lips moved imperceptibly, and I could hear her whisper, "Mehal, Mehal." They lay close to me, and I tried to touch them, but I could not. I woke up screaming, and drenched in sweat, and could not go back to sleep. On another occasion, I saw Luba, with her head shaven—just as it had been when she came back from the

121

hospital after recovering from typhoid fever—her face drawn, almost lifeless. I talked to her, but she would not answer. She looked at me with her gray eyes wide open, showing no interest in me. The nightmares revisited me almost nightly, depriving me of rest, and I would wake up in the morning, tired, walking like a zombie.

My confrontations with Ivan kept recurring; one evening, they became particularly violent. We had dinner in the mess hall, and Ivan recounted his sexual adventures. Turning serious, he explained that semen was produced in the male's breast, just as milk is produced in the female's. I sat opposite him a few seats away and could not help but snicker.

"What are you snickering about?!" he demanded, turning to me.

I was reluctant to start a fight, but said quietly that semen was produced in the testicle, to which everybody nodded approval. After dinner, on the way back to our barracks, Ivan caught up with me.

"Why did you embarrass me, you dirty little Jew?" he shouted with rage.

"I didn't mean to. I just wanted to straighten out the facts," I replied.

But Ivan did not want to debate. He began pounding me, hitting me with both fists on my face. I began kicking him with all my force, but he hit me harder yet, and I fell to the ground, unconscious. A few minutes later, Andrey, the sergeant, knelt over me, with a few other soldiers around.

"You're cut pretty badly near the eyes." he said. "Don't pick any fights! Stay away from that brute!"

I slowly got up and went to my bunk. Andrey came to see me a bit later, and told me he had had harsh words with Ivan and hoped he would behave. Then he reproached me impatiently: "You must learn how to fight back! Soon you may be confronting Germans in hand-to-hand combat. They are tougher than Ivan and neither I, nor anyone else, will be there to defend you."

In late March, the exercises became more strenuous. We had to march in full gear, 10 to 15 kilometers in the rain and mud, and return to the barracks in the dark. I would often be drenched and chilled when coming from the field. One evening, I developed a high fever and was sent to the infirmary. I had pneumonia, which the examining doctor considered dangerous. My one-week stay in the infirmary saved my life, as well as opened my eyes to the reality of the war.

The food in the infirmary was unforgettable: cutlets of veal, beef prepared goulash style (the way Mother used to do it), all sorts of salads and desserts. I had not eaten such food since I left home, three years earlier. It was certainly in sharp contrast to the regular evening meals of the last couple of months, mostly cabbage soup, with an occasional piece of meat. I soon turned the corner and began feeling better.

A young lieutenant sharing the infirmary with me introduced himself as Gregory Goldstein. I told him about my background, and in the next two days, the lieutenant and I did a lot of talking. I felt as if I had found a friend. Soon allowed to leave the infirmary for a few hours, Gregory introduced me to the officers' library. A new world of information was opened before me as I read daily and back issues of *Pravda* and *Izvestya*, as well as *Red Star*, the army's newspaper.

News of the United States and Britain engaged in heavy fighting in Italy near Monte Casino, of the British fighting the Japanese in Burma, and the United States major naval, air and infantry forces battling the Japanese all over the Pacific startled me. Most of the northern hemisphere—not just the Soviet Union—appeared in a huge conflagration whose outcome no one predicted with certainty, but would certainly determine the fate of the Western World for many decades, I thought. I often left the library with a foreboding reminding me of the day I left home.

I discovered the Soviets' ire with the United States for not opening the second front in the West, to divert some of the German armies from the Soviet Union, as apparently agreed upon by Stalin, Churchill, and Roosevelt.

I also found out, reading between the lines, that the Soviet army was experiencing heavy casualties. Although the retreating German armies were hurt fatally by the surrender of Von Paulus's army near Stalingrad and subsequent major defeats near Smolensk, they were still a formidable killing machine. They had heavily mined every road they abandoned, as well as the fields and forests in their paths. The Soviet army, lacking mechanical mine-sweepers, was forced to march soldiers through the mined fields, causing many deaths.

I read with horror accounts of massive graves of civilians killed by the Germans in Kiev, and other Ukrainian towns heavily populated by Jews. My heart sank, and I lost hope of ever again seeing my parents, relatives, and friends left in Dubno.

I shared my concerns with Gregory, who had access to other, more restricted army publications. He confirmed the heavy casualties the retreating Germans had been inflicting on the Soviet army. "The closer they come to their pre-war border, the tougher they get," he said. He expressed anger that the Allies had left the Soviets alone to fight Hitler. He hoped the Allies would keep their promises and open another front in Europe. He felt disappointed that, in the meantime, America had reduced delivery of vital equipment to replenish Soviet losses, claiming they needed to prepare their own forces for the invasion. "It is, unfortunately, a dangerous time to be a foot soldier, and I feel for you," the lieutenant said.

A week or so after I entered the infirmary, I returned to my barracks. Soon my comrades came back from the day's exercises in the fields and greeted me enthusiastically. When I got back to my bunk after dinner, Andrey visited me. Warm and friendly, he asked whether I would be ready to resume my soloist activities. He told me that Ivan had taken the soloist task back, but no one followed him in the refrain. I told Andrey I would be okay, but expressed concern that Ivan might again be angry with me.

"Let me worry about Ivan," he said, "you just do a good job."

The next day, as we marched out of the compound, I began a spirited military song and continued leading in the singing the rest of the day. After the meal, as I left the mess hall, Ivan caught up with me.

"You did it again, you dirty, little Jew!"

"Andrey asked me to do it."

Ivan was fuming. "It is you who betrayed a comrade, you little Judas. You could have told him you didn't want to sing."

Without waiting for my answer, he started hitting me, as hard as ever. I fell to the ground and lay there bleeding from the nose and mouth. People gathered around me, and soon Andrey appeared.

"I don't know what I'm going to do with you," he said sympathetically, as he leaned over me. "You've got to learn how to fight back."

He helped me get up, get to the bunk, brought me a towel soaked in cold water, and left. I reflected on what Andrey had said. How could I learn to defend myself? I had tried to fight Ivan, but I felt as if I were fighting a tree; he was so strong, towering over me, that I felt weak and helpless.

I learned later in the evening that Andrey put Ivan away for three days of confinement. When Ivan saw me after the confinement, he turned to me with eyes full of hatred and menace. "Wait until we get to the front. You'll be the first one that I'll try to get rid of!"

One evening, a week or two after the incident with Ivan, one of the soldiers in an adjoining bunk ran towards me. "Meesha, I have a surprise for you. Come with me."

He took me by the hand, dragging me out into the darkness to one of the compound's gates that were used in evenings for soldiers to exchange their rations of soap, cigarettes, and other amenities for homemade food to supplement the bland, meager food rations.

"Here is your sister!" my friend shouted with delight.

It was Luba! She looked much healthier than when I had left her three months earlier. Her face had filled out; her hair was longer. She had lost the "prisoner-out-of-jail" look that had followed her bout with typhoid fever. The sentry let me step outside. I sat down with Luba on a bench, and we began to talk.

"Why haven't you written to me, Mehal? You promised you would," she asked.

"I wrote to you every day. I haven't received an answer from you. I've worried so much. I thought I lost you and believed I was the only one left in the whole family."

"I see," she said after a minute of hesitation. "Something must be rotten in the State of Denmark. I tried to find out where you were and to get in touch with you, but to no avail. Mehal, you don't look so well, you're full of bruises, you've lost so much weight, and your eyes look sunken. What's happening to you?"

"I'm all right. Tell me about yourself. How did you get here?

How did you find me?"

"After you left, I decided to leave Sir Darya," Luba answered. She proceeded to tell me that Sergey helped her get the grain the collective farm owed us. He also arranged for her to travel once a week with the collective farm wagon to the farmers' fair to sell the grain. The worst part of it was walking back to Sir Darya from the market, some 10 kilometers away, with the money hidden in her clothes. After selling all the grain, she packed our belongings and left Sir Darya.

"How did you know to come here?" I asked.

"I saw the train which you had boarded in Sir Darya going west, and learning that there was a big military training compound near Kattaqurghan, I guessed that the train headed there," Luba said. She had arrived in Kattaqurghan two weeks earlier, and having inquired in town hall, she learned there were some people here from Dubno, one of them being Moniek Sadownik, a neighbor of ours. He helped her find a little room next to where he and his wife lived. She took a temporary job as a seamstress and began her search for me.

She lost all hope of finding me when the main office of the compound had denied that I was here. Persistent, she kept coming daily to watch and carefully inspect the troops marching out in the morning and returning in the evening. After ten days, she almost gave up in despair.

One evening, she recognized my voice as the soloist of a group returning to the compound. The following morning, she inquired at the headquarters again about me, insisting she knew that I was in the compound, but the officer she spoke to denied it. Finally, she came here to ask the soldiers whether they knew me, describing my looks and telling them I was a soloist. "So you see my efforts have paid off," she concluded, her voice breaking. She was silent for a while. Then: "Tell me more about yourself."

I described to Luba the training conditions, the barracks we stayed in, the food we ate. I also told her about my bout with pneumonia and the few violent encounters with Ivan. Late in the evening, the sentry asked me to come back in.

I went back to my bunk, but I could not sleep. What a sister, I thought, what a heroic woman! I became angry that my letters had probably never left the compound and were discarded, that Luba's inquiries by letter or in person were never answered, and that headquarters actually lied to her and denied my presence here. Suddenly, my loyalties to the country began to crack. Was the military hiding the truth to keep soldiers' families in the dark? Were the soldiers destined to become mine sweepers and their deaths hidden even from the closest of kin? This was not the country I felt ready to fight and die for I reflected with disappointment and alarm.

I saw Luba nearly every evening for the next few weeks. Then she failed to show up, and I became distraught: News spread that we would be leaving to the front in a week or so; I became concerned that I might not be able to say goodbye to Luba.

The martial training grew more intense the last week before the end of our tour. The training emphasized particularly hand-to-hand combat. I failed repeatedly in these encounters with my comrades, or even with dummies.

"You have to learn to hate before you attack to kill," Andrey would repeat to me. "You must be aware every second that either your enemy or you will die."

I tried to follow Andrey's instructions. I pictured in my mind challenging Ivan in combat, remembering how he hurt me and how angry he made me, calling me a dirty little Jew. But I could not muster enough hatred or anger to hurt my comrades now, and I could not imagine killing somebody.

Then came a real test. We were ordered to shoot at targets with bullets. Again I failed.

"You're not a fighter. You'll never learn how to fight!" Luba's warnings before we parted in Sir Darya rang in my ears.

When Luba came back a week later, "What happened, Luba?" I asked with alarm.

"I went to Samarkand. I just wanted to get the 'lay of the land!' I saw a number of people from Dubno, among them Asher Balaban—an upperclassman from the gymnasium—who is pretty high up in the government, a 'big shot.'"

"There is something urgent I need to tell you," I interrupted her. "Our unit will be leaving Kattaqurghan in three days, and probably sent to the front."

"That is why I went to Samarkand," she said. "I am a step ahead of you."

"What do you mean?" I asked.

"Let's talk about it when I see you next," she answered in a hushed voice. "Mehal, I have heard that the soldiers are allowed to visit their families before they leave for the front. I want you to get a permit to visit your sister. Will you do that?"

"All right," I said, as we parted.

Luba came back the next evening. My unit was scheduled to leave Kattaqurghan the day after. "Do you have the permit I told you to get?" she asked.

"Yes."

"Let us go to my place so we can talk more freely," Luba said.

Half an hour later, we came to her one-room apartment. "Sit down, relax, my brother," Luba said. "I want to talk to you, and I want you to listen very carefully. I have arranged for you to escape from the compound and from Kattaqurghan."

129

Her matter-of-fact pronouncement stunned me. "Do you know what you're saying?" I yelled. I told Luba that at the morning roll call, the colonel, head of the Kattaqurghan base, informing us of our imminent departure for the front, had drawn our attention to a soldier, allegedly a deserter, hanging by a rope from scaffolding. He warned that the same fate would befall anyone trying to desert from the army.

"Mehal," Luba answered, "I know what I tell you to do is very dangerous, but you going to the front is no less dangerous. I have tried to arrange everything for your safe escape. All I want you to do is to have a little faith and a little courage."

"But Luba, running away like that hurts me and my convictions. I have never committed a crime, and what you're asking me to do is criminal, punishable by death. And even if no one catches me, I will feel ashamed and guilty all my life," I protested.

"Mehal, I know how you feel, but you are not realistic. You think that you'll go to the front and kill a few Germans, avenging their mass murder of millions of innocents, possibly including our parents. However, you have never learned to fight, to hate, to murder somebody. You're short and thin—you're no match for a German soldier in combat. Besides, you'll probably be sent with hundreds of your comrades only to clear mines; you'll become a minesweeper," she said. "I heard in Samarkand that many soldiers have come back badly wounded, sometimes without limbs— blown up by mines. I don't want my brother to be blown up. I want you to live. You're probably the only remaining male member of Father's and Mother's families. You have a right to live; you have an obligation to live!"

I wanted to counter what Luba had said, but I froze and became speechless. Luba had used some of the same arguments a few months earlier, before I left for the army. Then, I had felt more sure of myself and more confident about my willingness to go to the army. But the last few months had taught me about my limitations and weaknesses. I could not stand up even to one Russian bully; how would I face a German soldier? I felt helpless and in a quandary. Maybe Luba was right; she had been right so often before, during the past three years.

Luba saw my hesitation and resumed her pleadings, more determined than before. "Mehal, we have no time to waste. There's a train leaving for Samarkand in an hour. If we don't catch that train, you'll have to return to the barracks and go to the front. Please listen to me. I want you to live. I want both of us to return home safely. Maybe we'll find our parents alive." She paused. "Take off your army uniform and put on the clothes I prepared for you." She trembled as she spoke, and her eyes filled with tears; she fixed her gaze, piercing my eyes. "Please listen to me, Mehal," she said softly. I listened to her, frozen, as if in a trance. I got up slowly and, as if forced by an invisible hand, I followed her command. In a few minutes, we were ready to go.

Luba had all her belongings packed in a bundle. She hid my uniform under the bed and tidied up the room. "Now let's run to the train station!" she said.

We went through the narrow, empty streets of Kattaqurghan and reached the train station. Luba handed me a train ticket that she had purchased earlier, and a new passport her friend in Samarkand, Asher Balaban, had prepared for me. Soon we boarded the train heading towards Samarkand.

"Follow my instructions carefully," Luba commanded sternly. We quickly went to the wagon next to the locomotive, and Luba approached the man shoveling coal into the engine furnace. "Don't you want to rest a bit? My brother will be glad to help you," she said, while she handed him a bundle of rubles. The man handed the shovel to me and I became an "engineering assistant." Luba took some coal dust and smeared it on my face. "Now you look like a real helper," she chuckled. Luba's maneuvers avoided the danger of a confrontation with the conductor, almost certainly an NKVD officer. A few hours later, at dawn of May 12, 1944, we arrived in Samarkand.

"Wait outside!" Luba commanded, as we disembarked and ran hastily towards the station. She came back a moment later with a wet rag and carefully wiped the soot off my face. We went inside the building and Luba took me by the hand. "You're trembling, Mehal, and you're very pale. Quiet down or you will alarm people around us," she whispered. "Sit down on the bench and wait here," she commanded. She left the belongings with me and ran out. A few minutes later she returned, motioning me to come with her. "Take us to the Old City," Luba said to the driver of a horse and buggy that she had hailed.

When we got to the main square, Luba directed the driver through narrow alleys to a small building, and paid him. We went up a flight of stairs, and Luba opened the door to a room she had rented for us. "This is going to be our home. It's not great, but I hope it will do for the time being."

CHAPTER 8

A Refugee in Samarkand –

The Weaver

The room Luba had rented was part of a building with small apartments for transients like us. Alas, overwhelmed with guilt, shame and fear, I made it difficult for us to stay there. I had committed a crime, punishable by death according to Soviet army code. Always the "good boy," obedient, ready to help, to give of myself, and to do good, I had never hurt anybody and had never broken the law. Overnight, I had become a criminal. I felt guilty that I had let Andrey down. He liked me and had been good to me, despite my being a Jew. Would he now think less of Jews? Would the whole brigade in Kattaqurghan become aware that a Jewish soldier had deserted? Beyond that, I felt guilty that I let down the host country that saved my life and that of Luba.

I felt ashamed that I had failed a real-life test, the ultimate test of willingness to give one's life to save the lives of many. Suddenly, I became aware of my limitations, lack of courage, and stamina. I had let my own people down, I thought harshly, having failed to fight their monstrous enemy.

The fear of being discovered overwhelmed me. The Polish proverb, "A thief will often stories sire, that his hat was on fire," kept haunting me. I felt as if the ground under me were on fire, and I wanted to run away, but where to? I feared the policeman on the street, as well as the letter carrier knocking on the door. I became suspicious of people's questions, and even their glances; my fears aroused suspicion among strangers and acquaintances alike.

I began to quarrel with Luba. "You orchestrated my AWOL!" I attacked her bitterly.

"You're behaving like a child!" she countered.

"You have made me feel like a traitor, like a nobody," I persisted.

"Take it easy, my brother. Everything will turn out all right."

Luba found a new place for us to stay, but my state of mind and behavior did not improve. She reproached me repeatedly, warning that I was arousing suspicion that would lead to my capture. "Mehal, our money is running low; you need to look for work, instead of grumbling to no end. You should go out and see how people are starving here. The price of a loaf of bread on the black market has nearly doubled in the couple weeks that we have been here. Wake up before we starve!" she erupted.

One day, I met through acquaintances a young man, Moniek Perlman, engaged in fixing machinery on a farm, who offered to take me with him as his assistant. He explained that my pay would consist mostly of grain which, he believed, would become essential for surviving the winter. I quickly agreed to join Moniek and work with him on a farm seven kilometers away. Luba cheerfully bid me goodbye, quoting an old Russian saying, "Don't worry, don't fret, joy and dancing will come our way yet." I noticed Moniek glancing at Luba and Luba smiling at him.

In his 20s, about my height, Moniek spoke with ease and excitement about his work. On the way to the farm, he told me about his younger years in Poland and the years in the Soviet

Union. He had been born and raised in an Orthodox Jewish family in Krakow, western Poland, now occupied by the Germans. He had attended *Yeshiva* schools for his Jewish education, but he had also a good secular education, mostly from his mother, and he avidly read classic books by Polish and Western European authors. Although he never finished high school, he had several patents to his name, including a major one pending for a redesign of the Polish telephone system. The war abruptly changed the course of his life.

He and his older brother, Joseph, had left their family and run east when the Germans invaded Poland in the fall of 1939 and went to Lvov. In the spring of 1940, the Soviet secret police apprehended Joseph and Moniek—among thousands of their compatriots—and sent them to a slave labor camp 500 kilometers north of Gorky.

Soon after Moniek and Joseph arrived in the camp, the weather turned extremely cold, with temperatures of -20 to -30 degrees. Many of the inmates suffered frozen limbs. Moniek and Joseph learned to prepare makeshift shoes from newspapers, and that saved their feet. The cold winter, the hunger, dysentery, and malaria in the summer depopulated the camp. Seven thousand inmates passed through the camp, but only a few hundred survived, Moniek told me.

Assigned to cut down trees in a huge forest, from early morning until dark, he conceived of an idea of installing a pulley-like arrangement on the back of a truck that was hauling the logs. One end of the pulley would be wrapped around a log and haul the log onto the truck. The head of the camp liked the idea and adopted it, though he made it known that it had been his idea, but he gave Moniek extra bread, just to keep him from telling the truth. "It was God's will that we survive," Moniek said.

In the late fall of 1941, an agreement between Stalin and General Wladyslaw Sikorski, head of the Polish government in London, committed the Polish army-in-exile, under General Wladyslaw Anders, to join the Allies' fight against the Germans. Stalin, in return, was to release all Polish prisoners. Moniek and Joseph left the camp and traveled by train to Samarkand. Joseph found work as a bookkeeper on a collective farm, and Moniek became a maintenance engineer on another collective farm, both within a few kilometers of Samarkand. Moniek used his inventive skills to devise an easy way of fixing machinery on the farm. He had been working on this collective farm for several months, staying at the farm weekdays, but visiting his friends in Samarkand on weekends and to celebrate the Sabbath.

We reached a hut, adjoining a barn, in the middle of the collective farm, and entered a small, corner room where Moniek stayed. The room, with a little window, barely letting in sunlight, had a cot where Moniek slept, and enough room for me to spread out on the dirt floor.

Shortly, we went out in the field and inspected a disabled combine for harvesting. Moniek explained that the collective farm had hardly any inventory of items or machinery to replace missing parts. Collective farms had strict allotments for new machinery and machinery parts, and each requisition of a new part had to be approved by a central agency in the Agricultural Department in Tashkent or, worse, in Moscow. Meanwhile, the urgency of harvesting the crops and the vegetables would create a panic to achieve the quotas imposed on the collective farm. The managers of the farms, as well as operators of the automated machinery, considered Moniek their savior, seeing him improvise, on the spur of the moment, replacement of broken or missing parts with similar or modified parts from another tractor or combine. He led me to other tractors and trucks waiting to be fixed, and instructed me to assist him in finding substitute parts from abandoned vehicles and machinery.

I became comfortable and felt at ease on the farm. My knowledge of the Uzbek language, though sparse, was adequate to communicate with the farmers. The weather was beautiful, the days balmy, and the nights mild.

The respite gave me an opportunity to rethink what I had learned about the Soviet Union. Norbert Wiener's short course on Soviet life served me well, as I observed the harsh struggle for survival of the people in Aksai and Sir Darya. I personally witnessed corruption on the farms where I served as veterinary assistant, as well as in Aksai, and its corrosive influence on the system and its people. Sergey's frightening account in Sir Darya about his relocation from Ukraine and loss of family; the failure of the government to inform next of kin about their young people fighting or dying at the front, confirmed Wiener's condemnation of the Communist regime's ruthlessness. I began to deeply doubt that I, or Luba, would want to stay in this country, even if given the opportunity to do so. Besides, I terribly missed my parents and became determined to return home with Luba; the sooner, the better.

A few weeks after my arrival on the farm, Moniek came back from Samarkand, excited with the news that the Allies had invaded the beaches of Normandy in France, opening another front in the war with a huge armada of aircraft and ships, and hundreds of thousands of men. The news thrilled me: Maybe we would soon all go home; maybe Mother and Father were all right, maybe we would be altogether again.

Later in the day, as we ate our modest meal of fruits and vegetables, Moniek revealed much sadder news he had heard on the radio and read in the newspapers, about the Soviet troops uncovering mass graves in towns abandoned by the Germans. The radio and press did not identify the victims, but we feared they were slaughtered Jews.

The news stunned me, and I feared for my parents' fate. And what about Grandma, Aunt Peshia and all my other relatives? Were they in any of those mass graves? I agonized. I shared my worries with Moniek.

"You should not assume the worst," he said. "You should have faith in God. Truly, the Almighty would not let us down. He saved us through the ages, and He'll save us again. Have faith!"

He expressed a stronger will than ever to live, to prosper, to give cogent meaning to life, and to be a good servant of God. I respected his deep faith. It certainly helped him to be at peace, to be more optimistic than me. However, his belief in a "God who saved us through the ages" sounded to me hollow and meaningless.

One Friday in July, I retrieved the grain I had carefully saved from my work on the farm and returned to Samarkand with Moniek, each of us carrying a grain-filled sack. He helped me locate Luba, who had moved to another part of the Old City.

"You look suntanned and healthy," Luba commented, as we unloaded a sack full of grain from the farm, and Moniek departed.

"I didn't get much pay, but this bundle should surely help," I said, gently embracing her.

The place Luba had rented, essentially an entry foyer to an Uzbek's dwelling, had a tiny room in the corner, which the owners had used for storage. Luba had transformed the foyer ingeniously into our living quarters, with a small stove and kettle, some wooden bowls and utensils, a small table, and a bench, all placed neatly along the outer wall. She equipped the little corner room with a large mat to sleep on, some old blankets, a small night table, and a kerosene lamp. I looked at everything with admiration and thankfulness.

"Luba, how did you manage to find this place and make it so beautiful?"

"A palace it isn't, but it will do," she answered.

Luba prepared a dinner of cabbage soup with potatoes and fresh fruit. After the meal, she told me about Jews who had escaped from Lodz and formed a cottage textile activity of weaving cloth and selling or bartering it to the local population. Lodz, the textile center of Poland before the war, consisted mostly of Jewish artisans and merchants. The Lodz Jews who had come here managed to build, with local carpenters, handlooms which they sold or rented to unemployed refugees and taught them to weave cloth. They also provided the yarn and the dyes for coloring the cloth. The Uzbeks loved the colorful material, which they used for making robes.

"So I thought that you and I could become clothes manufacturers. You'll do the weaving, and I'll do the selling," she concluded, smiling.

"You're wonderful, you are a wonderful dreamer," I replied. "And where will we get a loom? How will I learn to weave?"

She told me that she had arranged for me to spend a couple of weeks with a real master of the trade, to learn how to weave cloth on a handloom. Surprised but thankful, I agreed to start my training the following week.

The next Monday, Luba and I entered a large room with several looms in a hut, a block from ours. A short, middle-aged man named Aaron came out to greet us. He had red hair, reddish cheeks, blue eyes, and a lively face. Aaron, moving animatedly with authority, wore loose pants and a sweatshirt, and conveyed a businesslike air. "All right, Luba, you leave your brother here, and I'll put him to work. Let's not waste time." He pointed to the young men working at three looms, full of smiles and cheer. I shook their hands.

"Now, let me take you to my loom and introduce you to this wonderful machine. You see, Mehal, it is just a few planks put together, nothing to it, but it produces gold. Without this wonder machine, we would starve, just as many around us do."

The loom, framed like a table without a top, about five-feet wide, and eight-feet long, had a roller on each end. The roller at the near end held cotton fibers spread over its width, with hundreds of strands extending tautly like a sheet, and winding around the roller. At the further end, a cam, with hundreds of long needles, held up the strands with an upper-half of the sheaths, going through the eyes of the needles, lifting them from the main sheet. The cam was attached with brackets to two pedals; pressing one pedal lifted the cam, pressing the other pedal lowered the cam through the strands of the main sheet.

A pulley attached above the loom directed the motion of a shuttle, a mouse-like device containing a spool of thread. Pulling the handle of the pulley propelled the shuttle, laying a thread across the sheet of strands. Dispatching the shuttle in the reverse direction would lay another thread across. Moving the cam to and fro would secure each vertical thread and create new material.

Aaron invited me to sit next to him on the bench and asked me to practice moving the pedals up and down with my feet, and to move the cam to and fro. Then he handed the pulley to me, commanding that I pull it down firmly. I yanked the pulley and the shuttle went flying out of the channel.

"Well, you need to jerk it, but not as hard. You need a little practice," Aaron said. He proceeded to give me exercises. After a few days, I was able to start producing material, albeit very slowly, very carefully. Furthermore, the material had lots of wrinkles and the edges were uneven. Two weeks after my arrival, Aaron, satisfied with my proficiency at the loom, dismissed me and asked that I revisit him evenings as often as I could, to learn other aspects of the trade.

"I think I'm ready to become a weaver," I boasted to Luba, returning home. "At least Aaron thinks so." Luba told me she had found new friends who lived nearby—a rabbi and his wife, Esther Zuckerman, who happened to be Aaron's cousin, and who would like me to work for them.

I burst out laughing, "You're a magician, Luba. Watch out! They might arrest you for witchcraft."

The next day I met the Zuckermans. Rabbi Zuckerman, slight, of average height, looking in his 60s, wore a cylindrical, dark skull cap on his gray, nearly bald head, thick eyeglasses, and sported a beard with short, thin, white hair. He shook my hand warmly and he greeted me in Yiddish. "Good to meet you, Mehal. Luba tells me that you have finished training with Aaron. You know, he's the dean of Samarkand weavers, and if he says you're good, I'm sure you are. I hope you'll like working with us.

"You know, it's funny. Making a living here is illegal. If they catch us, they'll send us to Siberia as capitalists. Living in poverty, starving to death, that is permissible, but preparing clothes for the people to wear is forbidden! It's a great state we live in." Then, as an afterthought, he resumed: "Still, it's better than being killed by the Germans, so let's thank God for that. Just be careful and don't talk about it. We're happy to have you."

Then he introduced me to his wife, Esther, a short, light-skinned and dark-haired woman, amazingly resembling my mother. She greeted us warmly and asked that we join them for breakfast. She told us they had lost a young man who had worked for them for a while, and then decided to join his brother and form their own business. Rabbi Zuckerman recounted their life in the Soviet Union. They had fled Bessarabia, Romania, at the beginning of Germany's onslaught on the Soviets in the summer of 1941, and had come to Samarkand, essentially taking the same route that we had. But coming two years earlier, they were well-established by now.

The rabbi interspersed his account with sarcasm and ridicule of the government, making it clear to me that he hated the Soviets. He spoke with conviction and vehemence, as if driven by a force he could not control. I believed that he was an honest man and knew much more about Soviet life than I did, and his words began to resonate with me.

After breakfast, Luba left for work, teaching in the local school. I ensconced myself at the new cedar-wood loom, which emitted fresh scents that teased my senses. The sheath of threads stretched before me, multicolored stripes that shimmered in the morning sun scintillating through the window. I moved the pulley and the pedals with ease, and felt excited to be useful and productive. Working at full speed, I had made 15 meters of new cloth by the end of the day. That would sell for quite a bit, I thought.

Life moved on, with new meaning and a new rhythm, and I felt as if airborne when I went back to see Aaron. "My, my, you look like a new man! Life must be treating you all right," Aaron greeted me. I told Aaron about my work, and that I was anxious to take him up on his offer to learn more about my new vocation. He spent a few hours showing me patiently how to pull hundreds of strands through the eyelids of the cam, and how to fasten them at the base of the roller. He told me how to interlace different colors of the strands, to prepare more colorful material. He also explained the basic steps of dyeing and drying the yarn.

In September 1944, the Uzbek Economic Institute announced the start of a new academic year, and I decided to enroll for evening classes. I had to take an entrance exam, since I did not have any documents to prove my previous education. A week later, I became a student of the Institute, attending classes three evenings a week, after day-long work at the loom.

My walks to the Institute in the New City, a few kilometers from where we lived, opened a new world for me. The Old City, overcrowded, with narrow dirt roads and winding alleys among dilapidated huts, filthy, noisy, and dusty, conveyed an odor of decay and a sense of poverty.

The new part of Samarkand had wide streets with sidewalks, solid multi-storied buildings, large parks, and banks near the Zerafshan River. The Uzbeks and the refugees lived in the Old City; the Russians, the officials, the professors at the university, and other professionals lived in the New City.

On my way to the Institute, I walked past a number of museums and mosques, the most impressive being the Mausoleum of Tamerlane, with its colorful, mosaic-glazed tiles glistening brightly in the sun, as if newly laid. Learning that the building dated back to the 14th century, when Tamerlane, the famed conqueror, had swept the region and established Samarkand as his capital, astonished me. Tamerlane and his descendants rebuilt and beautified the city, whose beginnings went back to over 2000 years, to the time of the birth of Athens and Rome. Legend had it that Alexander the Great extolled its beauty, calling it the Jewel of the East.

I learned that Samarkand, located at an important crossroad between Persia, Turkey, and China, served as the center of the Silk Route, and had a colorful, and often tragic, history. In the 8th century, the city had come under Arab domination. Early in the

The Weaver

13th century, Genghis Khan and his Mongol hordes invaded and ruined the city, chasing out and killing most of its inhabitants. The city had a rebirth under Tamerlane, and it prospered for several centuries before being torn by strife and wars. In the late

19th century, the Russians overwhelmed the whole region. Throughout the upheavals of 1200 years since the Arabs' conquest, the city remained essentially Muslim.

Two months had passed since I began working for the Zuckermans. Esther and Luba became close friends and, indeed, Esther treated both of us as if we were part of her family, often inviting us to partake delicious Sabbath meals. The Zuckermans also treated us well financially, and we began to save money.

"Mehal, I think we should buy our own loom and have our own business," Luba said one evening. I protested that the Zuckermans treated us well and I should not walk out on them. I also expressed concern that we should not spend all our savings buying a loom. Luba assured me that she found a good worker to replace me at the Zuckermans and felt certain we could buy a loom mostly on credit.

A week later, Luba delivered on her promises. The Zuckermans, happy to see us do well, assured us that the new man Luba had found for them appeared capable and eager to work. "It will be our greatest pleasure to see you prosper."

Luba found an inexpensive second-hand loom, which we put in our small corner room. The loom took up most of the space in the room, leaving only a small area, no more than four-by-ten feet for our living quarters. The loom became my constant companion. I would start work at 6 a.m. and work until dusk, with the exception of the three nights when I would visit the Institute.

Soon, with Aaron's help, Luba and I learned to prepare the cotton sheaths. We bought a big kettle in which we boiled water and added the proper dye. We placed the cotton bale in the colored water, and then dried out the cotton. I learned how to secure the cotton strands on the loom and thread the strands

Tamerlane's Tomb

through the needles of the cam. Furthermore, we interspersed bales of different colors with bands of white to provide an attractive longitudinal design.

I produced, on the average, 20 meters a day of colorful cloth, which Luba wrapped herself with, putting a raincoat on top, and proceeded with it to the "black market," a place in hidden alleys, hopefully away from the watchful eyes of the NKVD.

There, she exchanged the material for fresh produce or sometimes rubles or occasional dollars. We became "professional" weavers and owners of a profitable enterprise.

I attended the Institute regularly, but I had limited time to study or to read assignments. I compensated by being attentive to the lectures and avidly absorbing the material in class. Sometimes I would return home in the evening and review my notes by candlelight, with the help of a textbook I could occasionally borrow from the Institute library. My exam scores reflected my effort: I got nearly perfect scores, and my professors praised me for my classroom participation.

In January 1945, the weather turned particularly cold for this part of Uzbekistan. Food grew much scarcer, the small rations of bread and meager necessities were being reduced, and long queues of people waiting for their rations were often turned away. Typhoid and other infectious diseases spread though the town.

Rumor had it that America, now busy supplying its own troops, who were engaged in bitter fighting with the Germans on the Western Front, diminished its former largesse to the Soviet Union. Yet, the need for warmer clothing in the cold weather, as well as for other necessities, had increased. Our small enterprise actually prospered, despite deteriorating conditions in the city.

March 1945 brought good news from all fronts. The Soviet army was moving into Germany proper and advancing towards Berlin. The allies had eliminated the Germans' threat of encirclement at the Battle of the Bulge and were advancing eastward towards Germany.

Moniek's visits became more frequent, transforming Luba into an animated, happy, young woman. I noticed her excitement when Moniek came to visit and her radiant joy upon returning from an evening out with him. Luba was falling in love, I thought, delighted to see her happy. A bit jealous, I felt my time would come as well. Meanwhile, preoccupied with work and studies, I felt proud and satisfied that I provided sustenance for Luba and myself, as well as savings for the future. Indeed, the future became pregnant with hope and promise to me, as news of imminent end of the war filled the air.

"The war is over! The war is over!" Rabbi Zuckerman yelled, bursting into our hut at dusk, flushed with excitement, on May 9, 1945. "We just heard it on the radio. The Germans capitulated. Hitler committed suicide!"

We were intoxicated with joy: After so much suffering and so many deaths, the war was over and the monster gone! After years of living in filth, covered with vermin, I felt as if a warm shower had washed it all off and made me clean again.

We went with the Zuckermans to their hut and were glued to the radio, listening to breaking stories and commentaries on the exciting news until early morning. Then, exhausted, we began to worry whether our families had survived.

Moniek had written home to Krakow to let his family know that he and his brother were in Samarkand. In mid-June, Moniek received a brief note from his mother: "I have survived, Father did not. I'm thrilled that you and Joseph are okay. Come home soon."

"We must hurry and go back home," Moniek said after a while, regaining his composure.

Luba had written many letters to Dubno Town Hall, but we had received no reply. Newspapers reported that the Red Army kept discovering more mass graves in western Ukraine. Worries about our parents haunted and saddened me. We received no news of Hershl's whereabouts either; nearly four years had gone by since his disappearance, and Luba's many inquiries had remained unanswered. We hoped for the best, but feared the worst.

Meanwhile, Joseph, Moniek's older brother by some seven years, married Leena, a refugee from Krakow who lived alone, having lost her parents to typhoid fever the previous winter. The couple moved to the collective farm where Joseph had been working as an accountant.

On August 6, 1945, the United States ushered in a new age of waging war, as it dropped an atomic bomb on Hiroshima. The destructive power of the new weapon suddenly propelled the United States as the most potent and feared superpower. The second atom bomb, dropped three days later, convinced the Japanese to surrender, and World War II came to an end.

Soon Luba and I decided to return home. Luba, ecstatic, told me that Moniek would like to join us; however, Joseph and Leena would like to stay behind a week or two longer to settle their affairs. Joseph's superior at the farm arranged permits for us to leave Samarkand. We sold our loom, packed our meager belongings, and began our journey back home.

CHAPTER 9

Going Home – Home No More

In September 1945, Moniek, Luba, and I boarded a train to Krasnovodsk in Turkmenistan, on the eastern shore of the Caspian Sea. This time, we did not need to avoid armed sentries or jump onto a moving train, since we had purchased our tickets and obtained papers, albeit illegally, through the good offices of Joseph's superior at the farm.

I was excited and full of hope: Maybe my parents did manage to survive, and would it not be wonderful to see Sophie again! My heartbeat quickened as I saw her as clearly as on the day we had parted amid the falling bombs.

Two days later, we arrived in Krasnovodsk. The following day, we secured a boat to cross the Caspian Sea and land in Baku, on the sea's western shore. From there, we went by train to Odessa, a port on the Black Sea. This gave us our first shock. Odessa, nearly half of whose inhabitants had been Jewish before the war, appeared to be free of Jews. We soon learned from passengers at the station that all the Jews had been killed. Our stop in Kiev a few days later confirmed the horrific truth. Most of Kiev's Jews had been shot and buried in a ravine called Babi Yar.

Finally, we arrived in Lvov, the main city of southeastern Poland, with a population of several hundred-thousand, of whom about half had been Jewish before the German invasion. We soon found a synagogue that was open for refugees, and secured a small corner in one of the rooms, with two benches to sleep on. Moniek and I shared one of the wider benches. In the middle of the night, Luba tugged me by my shirt.

"You go and sleep on my bench, Mehal," she whispered. I saw love piercing through her eyes and a steely determination to be with her man, and I obliged.

Next morning, Moniek explained that he and Luba decided to get married, and he immediately wanted to find a rabbi. Later in the day, I witnessed the rabbi perform the wedding of Moniek and Luba. Another witness, a thin man in his 30s, introduced himself as Yakov Hirsh from Dubno, our hometown.

"I knew your parents in the ghetto," he said to Luba. "I'll speak to you after the wedding. *Mazel Tov! Mazel Tov!*"

I looked at the eyes of the newlyweds, and though overcome with emotion, I felt much more secure and hopeful, as the rabbi led us to a small room to have some refreshments, and left.

"What is the matter Luba?" I asked, seeing her in Moniek's arms, crying.

"Where's Mother? Where's Father to be here with me?" she replied, continuing to sob. "I'll be all right, Mehal, don't worry."

Half an hour later as we lingered, Yakov came back, accompanied by an attractive, well-dressed woman who introduced herself as Sarah Gochberg. "Do you remember me? We were classmates."

"Oh yes! I remember very well," Luba answered, and they embraced. Not much taller than Luba, she had red hair, lots of freckles on her face, lively green eyes, and a warm smile.

We picked up our few belongings and left the synagogue, with Sarah and Yakov leading the way. A few minutes later, we climbed two flights of stairs in a large brick building, and Sarah opened the

The author and his sister, Luba, in 1945.

door to her apartment.

"Come in, come in, make yourselves comfortable," she said, and she took us on a tour of her spacious apartment.

"This is beautiful," Luba said, "How did you get such a gorgeous apartment?"

"Come into the kitchen. Relax, and I'll tell you everything," Sarah said.

Sarah prepared tea and pastries, and began telling us about the horrors of Dubno. On the fifth or sixth day after their arrival, the Germans gathered the best-known Jews of Dubno—the two rabbis, well-to-do businessmen, about 100 professionals—and hanged them in the middle of the market square. A few weeks later, they ordered all Jews to wear yellow bands with the Star of David. Soon after that, they began to apprehend Jewish women at random and haul them away. On *Simhat Torah,* they organized the first "action"; they picked up hundreds of young people, took them to the Jewish cemetery, shot them, and buried them in deep ditches.

Towards the end of 1941, the Germans set up a ghetto, enclosing the streets of Berka Yoselevicza, Stara, and a couple more. Then they began to starve the Jews, reducing the rations of bread and eliminating all other food. Yet the Jews had to perform heavy work for long hours. Sarah worked as a seamstress from dawn to evening. The winter months brought cold, famine, and illness, and many of the old and the very young were dying. This was followed by mass executions to liquidate the ghetto.

In April 1942, during Passover, the Germans, with the help of Ukrainian *Gendarmes*, cordoned off a third or so of the ghetto at night. They forced all the Jews from the segregated area into the streets and hauled them, by foot and on trucks, outside the town, into a ravine near the river. There, they forced the men to dig ditches, telling them it was for anti-aircraft defense. When the ditches were complete, they lined up rows upon rows of the Jews, machine-gunned them, and with bulldozers, pushed the victims into the pits, covering them with the dug-out earth.

A few people had escaped and come back to the ghetto to tell about the atrocities. That's when Sarah's mother and father ordered her to leave the ghetto. "I'll tell you more later about my miraculous survival. Let us first have something to eat," Sarah suggested.

Sarah's story left me in shock. I had read about German atrocities, and I had feared the worst. But this personal account from a survivor pained me with an intensity I had not experienced before. The horror of hearing this awakened me to a new, dark reality that Mother and Father and all my relatives were dead.

"I hope you can stay here for a while with us," Sarah said. "Now, go and wash up and I'll prepare dinner."

"My name is Sasha," a young man introduced himself, as Sarah led us to the kitchen.

"This is my husband," Sarah said with pride. Sasha, a handsome man in his 30s, explained that he had come from Odessa and met Sarah in Lvov, while serving as a colonel in the Red Army. Presently, he engaged in trading goods with friends in Odessa.

Sarah prepared a beautiful dinner for us. "You deserve a decent meal after the wedding," she exclaimed. She brought in a first course of broiled fish. The meal continued with meat, vegetables, and potatoes and ended with dessert.

During dinner, Yakov told us that when the Germans set up the ghetto, our home became the housing for 20 or so people, and he and his parents were among them. Also among the 20 were our grandmother, our aunt with her little boy, our uncle, his wife and their two daughters, and several of Father's relatives.

One day, after the first wave of executions, our parents left the ghetto to reach our father's friend, a Ukrainian, in a village near Dubno. Towards evening, they returned with Mother near collapse. A young SS man named Hoffman had recognized Mother and turned our parents back, whipping them on the way. According to Mother, Hoffman, a classmate of Luba, sometimes visited our home.

"Yes, yes, I remember him. So when did he join the SS?" Luba asked.

"That I can't tell you," Yakov answered. "But I know that many young people, particularly of German extraction—and Hoffman must have been German—eagerly joined the SS." This incident convinced our parents to stay in their home.

Three months after that, the Germans went through another

action. This time, they decided to get rid of all older people and young children, any and all Jews who were not able to work. They swept through the remaining part of the ghetto and hauled away about 3000 people, among them our grandmother, our aunt, her little boy and several of Father's elderly relatives, leaving only Avrum, his wife, our parents, Yakov's parents, and Yakov. Father wanted to run away, repeating that he wanted to see his children again, but Mother refused to leave.

Shortly after the second wave of killings, Father decided to build an underground bunker. He explained the bunker would go from the cellar of the house to the end of the property and have an opening in the adjoining lumberyard. So the group started digging, mostly in the evening, after returning from work and at night; every day another foot or two. It was back-breaking work, but the group managed to complete quite a bit of the bunker, well-hidden in the cellar.

In late September, it had become apparent the Germans would kill all remaining Jews. Yakov's parents, as well as our father, urged Yakov to flee the ghetto. Yakov made his way to the woods, some ten miles from Dubno, and spent the remaining year-and-a-half with a group of other young Jewish men and women in the forest, rummaging the fields at night for food. Winter brought death to several of the group; nevertheless, a dozen of them managed to survive until the Russians came in February 1944. The Germans killed the remaining 5000 Jews in October, on *Simchat Torah,* and liquidated the ghetto.

We listened in silence, though Luba cried quietly. I felt a throbbing pain as I pictured my parents, emaciated and weak, embracing each other as they were awaiting execution. They appeared frozen, yet at peace with each other. They stood vividly before me, so close I thought I could touch them. I felt remorse at not being with Mother and Father when they needed me most.

"Some way to greet young honeymooners," Sasha interrupted. "Yes, what the Germans did is enough to make you lose your faith in man and hope for the future. But, we must go on living and slowly heal the wounds. Let's retire. We'll have plenty of time to talk more tomorrow, and the day after, and the day after." We got up, and I gently embraced a shivering, whimpering Luba, as we parted for the night.

The next few days, we learned the unbelievable story of Sarah's survival. After the first wave of executions in the spring of 1942, Sarah's parents made arrangements with a Czech family to find shelter for her. One evening, Sarah took a small bundle of belongings and all the money and jewelry her parents had, and left the ghetto. The Czech, a business friend of her father's, met her at an appointed place and accompanied her to the home of an elderly couple, who made arrangements for her to stay in their home's attic.

The attic had a little opening which could be reached only by ladder. The couple delivered to Sarah morning and evening meals, and emptied her chamber pot. She had to be absolutely quiet, and when she cried, which she did a lot, she was to pack her mouth with a towel. She found it hardest of all to fight off loneliness and sadness, and to keep her sanity. She lost track of time. Finally, in the spring of 1944, she heard commotion and shouting: "The Russians are here!"

Released from her "prison," she found no Jews in Dubno, and she feared for her life, her home having been taken over by Ukrainians. Slowly and dangerously, she made her way to Lvov, where she met Sasha.

As I listened to the accounts of this catastrophe, I felt as if I were in a land of insanity. Where did such hatred, such beastliness, come from? The air and the earth's soil appeared to me filled with poison, and I concluded that we could not stay in Lvov, nor elsewhere in Ukraine or Poland.

A week following the wedding of Luba and Moniek, Joseph and Leena arrived, but soon departed for Krakow, eager to join Joseph's mother and relatives who had survived the war. Moniek, Luba, and I stayed, and during the next few weeks, we learned about the death of the Jewish community, the murder of nearly 200,000 Jews through open-air executions, and in two death camps near Lvov. Lvov, the largest city in the part of Ukraine west of the pre-1939 Russian-Polish border, also had the largest Jewish population, which, between 1939 and 1941, swelled with a large wave of refugees from German-occupied Poland. Barely a few thousand Jews had survived the slaughter.

Despite the calamity, Jewish life began to stir again in Lvov. Jews who had escaped to Russia ahead of the Germans were returning, and began to build a new, though fragile, life. Synagogues and charitable institutions tried feverishly to help returning Jews find temporary shelter, as well as to reclaim their property. But the survivors' urge to go to Palestine and build a Jewish home began to dominate their plans and thoughts. Their stay in Lvov was temporary and not without fear.

"Beware of the Ukrainians!" people warned us. "They were more brutal than the Germans, and they still are. They have stolen Jewish property, and they fear the returning Jews will try to take it back," we were told. People also warned us that Jewish life in the smaller towns had been completely extinguished. Furthermore, travel outside Lvov posed great danger, as Ukrainian partisans, fighting the Russians, roamed the roads, eager as ever to kill more Jews.

In October 1945, Luba, Moniek, and I decided to begin our

trek home to Dubno, despite the warnings of dangerous travel conditions. We had planned to go by train, but found it impossible to get permits. We waited at the main road going north from Lvov, and had the good fortune of waving down a truck driver, who agreed to drop us off in Dubno, on his way further north to Rovno, in return for a sum of money.

CHAPTER 10

Coming Home – Bearing Witness

Homecoming to Dubno
There lived once a Shtetl here
Where I was born and raised,
On a hill, resplendent, shone the Great Synagogue
Where I sang in its choir God's praise.
Much lore and culture flourished here
With preachers the world revered
A market thrived once in my Shtetl
And throngs who'd sell and buy
The stores had all been boarded up
The Shtetl and its people had died.
I knocked on the door of my humble home
Anxious its state to view
A man with a pitchfork sprang forth and yelled,
"Get out, you dirty Jew!"
"You are a thief, a monster!" – I fumed –
"You've stolen my home, you brute!"
I walked the lonely streets in distress
Anger gripping my breast.
I met a survivor who embraced me and urged:
"Go 'n see the valley of death."
Along the banks of the Ikva River

Beneath a rolling knoll
Skulls and limbs screamed death all around
Casting a chilling pall.
I seethed with rage as I gazed transfixed,
At the horror of the curse of old.
Here, for a thousand feet and beyond,
Lay the remains of all:
My parents, grandmother, relatives, and friends
And eight-thousand sacred souls.

Refrain: Don't cry, my soul
Don't bleed, my heart
Your mourning is all in vain
The venom of hate
Envy and greed
Has turned the world insane.

A chilly, gray, rainy afternoon greeted us as we arrived in Dubno and proceeded to our home, a kilometer or so away from the main road. We quickened our pace in anticipation of seeing our home, as we walked through cobblestone, empty streets. The house, on Berka Yoselevicza, number 256, looked worn and shabby, its pink paint peeled, the brick front entrance filled with weeds, and its little fence broken.

"Let me try to enter," Luba suggested.

Moniek and I stayed behind as she climbed the few steps and knocked on the door. "What do you want?" shouted a short, skinny man, in Ukrainian, opening the door.

"I want to just take a look at the house I used to live in," Luba said quietly.

The man slammed the door in her face. Luba came down and

rejoined us, with tears in her eyes. Choked with anger, I had a feeling that the Ukrainians who lived in our home might have helped the Germans in their grisly task of killing my parents.

"We better find another place to stay before it gets dark. Let's go to Uncle Avrum's place," Luba said.

We knocked, with some hesitation, on the door of Uncle's much larger home, a block from ours, fearing another Ukrainian would chase us away. A short, stocky woman greeted us warmly. We introduced ourselves.

"My name is Rivka Chayat, I am a sister of Gitl Guberman, Avrum's wife," she said, and she invited us to the living room, where we met her husband, Jacob. "You must be freezing. Let me have your wet coats. Sit down and warm up." She excused herself and soon returned with tea and pastries.

We told Rivka and Jacob briefly about our last four years in the Soviet Union. She told us about her miraculous survival with a peasant family, her return to Dubno to reclaim her sister's home, and meeting and marrying Jacob. "Unfortunately, there are hardly any Jews left in Dubno. The Germans killed all of them. That includes my sister and her family, as well as your parents and all your parents' relatives. And now, I'm not sure whether we should stay here either."

Rivka prepared dinner for us, and then showed us around the house and invited us to stay in one of the bedrooms. Before retiring, Rivka suggested that we try to obtain, from the town administrator, proper documents of ownership of our home, as well as of Grandmother's house. Luba decided to visit town hall next day; I said that I would like to browse around town. After a fitful night, I got up early and found Rivka in the kitchen; she served me a light breakfast. I bid her goodbye and left on my solitary tour.

The street, quiet and empty, appeared devoid of life. I remembered it being filled with children going to school and people rushing to work in early hours of the morning. It felt eerie, as if I had been transported to a vacuum chamber. My pulse raced as I walked west, approaching my old home where, a day earlier, the Ukrainian had slammed the door in Luba's face.

Memories of the past flooded my mind, as I stood in front of the shabby house that had been my home before the war. The acacia tree was still there, in front of the house, with the little bench around it, where Luba used to sit and read for hours in the summer. The barely visible remains of the vegetable garden in the yard brought recollections of Father and me tilling the small plot and planting cucumbers, tomatoes, lettuce, cabbage, scallions, squash, and sunflowers. I remembered the joy of seeing the plantings grow and the vegetables ripen.

I felt a bitter sweetness seeing the place of my birth where I spent my childhood and teenage years, now rumpled and messy. Grief overcame me and I felt weakness in my limbs, as if drained of strength; I choked with tears. All the anger and anguish of the past few weeks poisoned my innards and drove me to insanity. A darkness, a deep sadness, overwhelmed and paralyzed me. I leaned against the broken fence and broke out convulsively sobbing. I felt so alone.

A thought occurred to me—I would pay a visit to the Ukrainian, under the pretext of trying to buy his house. I knocked on the front door, and the Ukrainian appeared; I told him I wanted to take a look at the house and offer him a sum of money to buy it. He asked me to wait. Then he came out with a pitchfork, yelling: "Get out, you dirty, little Jew, before I kill you."

"You are a thief," I screamed. "You have stolen my home," and I left.

I seethed with rage, and a wild idea obsessed me. I went west on Berka Yoselevicza and found the small passageway I had used for a shortcut to the high school. I waited at the corner and saw the Ukrainian leave our home. I went back, took a stone from the broken sidewalk, and hurled it with all my force through the large window of the room which Luba and I had shared. Then I ran back through the passageway to Panienska. I hid in the corner of a house, but no one came in pursuit. Then, as if released from a pressure cooker, I leaned against the cold stone and began sobbing. "Tatte," I cried, "you never told me there was so much evil in the world!"

A while later, I went back to Berka Yoselevicza, knocking in vain on the doors of the neighboring homes, some abandoned and boarded up. I wondered what had happened to Hayim, Motel, Joseph, Jacob, Nathan, and David; had they survived the war? I proceeded west past the first grammar school and remembered the history teacher's assurances of a better world to come, thanks to the French Revolution ushering in an era of freedom, fraternity, and equality.

A few hundred yards further, I passed the old *Tarbut* grammar school I had attended eight years earlier, now in complete disrepair. The teacher of Jewish history, a devoted Zionist, came to life before me, pleading that we all go to Palestine to build a Jewish home. His voice, full of passion, reverberated in my ears: "There is no future for Jewish, young people in Poland or anywhere else, except in Palestine."

I continued on Berka Yoselevicza and knocked on the doors of my school friends' homes. Hearing no response, I turned left on Aleksandrowica and headed south, past Panienska, the town's main street, and found, next to the corner, the boarded-up store where my parents had had their soft-goods business before the war.

165

Further south, I reached Sophie's home. I was short of breath, with a choking sensation in my throat, as I opened the latch to the backyard. Sophie's voice still rang as clearly as on the day I asked her, four years earlier, to run away with me and Luba: "You talk like a true teenager. You make it sound like a picnic. Do you have an address to go to?"

I went up onto the porch and knocked on the door, but to no avail. I looked through the window and saw the furniture that had been there on the day I parted with Sophie. I wondered what might have happened to Sophie: Did the Germans or Ukrainians kill her or did she die from starvation or illness? I wondered what Sophie would have become if she had lived. I felt angry that the brutes had killed this beautiful, talented, and brilliant young woman, just as they had killed all the other Jews of Dubno.

I went to the high school, on the same route Sophie and I used to take, as we walked to school. I found the small wooden table and a bench where I had sat painting the castle, once the symbol of Dubno's military prowess of centuries past. A massive fort with cannon posts guarding its long perimeter, with a red ceramic roof, built on an island of the Ikva River, and the bridge leading to its entry across a moat, the structure appeared abandoned now.

Sounds I remembered from the high school reverberated in my ears, lingering laughter from the last two years preceding the war, years filled with hope and dreams of a new life under Communism. Communism would bring eternal peace and well-being to all people, I remembered my teacher of Marxism-Leninism assuring us in the classroom. Another misguided idea, I thought, having witnessed the corruption and injustice in the Soviet Union. Though tempted to enter the high school building, I feared that some of the teachers might have collaborated with the Germans to kill off my people, and I decided not to.

I turned around, heading east, and made my way to Panienska to visit Grandmother's house. The house dated to the early 1800s, having been built by my great-grandparents who had supplied provisions to General Suvorov's army during the Napoleonic Wars and thereby earned the Suvorkhi nickname. I had spent many hours perusing the files of my grandfather's commercial transactions, and possibly of the earlier generations of Gubermans, dealing with hops, flour, and grain, in addition to meat. Grandmother's tales of her years of suffering and her struggles to feed her two sons and four younger daughters, with Peshia barely a child, crossed my mind.

I knocked on the front door of the portion of the spacious house my grandmother had lived in, and a middle-aged woman suspiciously greeted me. I explained my relationship to the house's owner, and she invited me in. I recognized, and expressed surprise, that the layout and furnishings of the house looked the same as it had before the war. The woman told me that German officers had occupied the house, and she and her husband, a Soviet official, had been living in the apartment for over a year. Another Soviet official occupied the other part of the house, she mentioned. I briefly recounted my war experiences and left.

Luba greeted me cheerfully when I returned to Uncle's home. "If we're lucky, we might be able to sell our home." She told me that the town hall official record-keeper was able to verify our ownership of the house, and he promised to process appropriate papers in the next few days. "I'm going to try to do the same for Grandma's house," Luba said enthusiastically.

A few days after our arrival, Joseph Gitman, son of one of the two official rabbis in town, came to Dubno. He had studied in the late '30s at *Tahkemoni*, the famous liberal rabbinic school in Warsaw. He had returned home from Warsaw just before the war

167

started and had become a teacher in the high school. A distant relative on my mother's side, he had taken a liking to Luba, and they had seen each other for a while, but Luba did not care for him.

After the German invasion in June of 1941, Joseph ran away and landed in Tashkent, Uzbekistan's capital; at the end of the war he made his way to Dubno, taking similar routes to ours. Joseph found a place to stay with a distant relative who had survived the war and regained his home.

I liked Joseph and felt a kinship with him, and we began to take long walks around town. A kilometer north of our home, two boarded-up, broken structures stood as stark reminders of the catastrophe. Joseph's father, the rabbi, led the congregation in the larger structure, a bustling house of prayer. The smaller house of prayer, named after the rebbe of Tritsk, was the house of prayers for several hundred congregants, including my family. More than that, it served also as the small *Yeshiva* (Talmudic School), where I joined several dozen other young men in afternoon studies of the *Talmud*, commentaries on the Bible.

The sing-song voice of the stern rabbi interpreting the text rang in my ears, as I remembered his angular, stark face with its thinned-out, white beard. I remembered, too, the throngs that on the holidays filled the hall with the passionate prayer: "I shall not die but live and tell of the wonders of God." I felt a pain traverse my chest, as I thought of my good, devoted rabbi and my friends in the Yeshiva; I wonder if any of them survived the slaughter.

Our visit to the Great Synagogue, a block away, brought sweet memories. The synagogue, an imposing structure seen for miles around, had been built a hundred years earlier, at the height of Jewish prosperity in Dubno. "What happened to the synagogue?" we asked the sentry in front of the closed door.

"The Germans used it as a stable," the sentry said. "Now the town is trying to clean it out and make some use of it."

I remembered singing in the choir of the famed Chazzan Zalman Sherman: *Haben Yakir Lee Ephrayim* (I will remember my dear son, Ephrayim). Cantor Sherman stood me on a chair so that the High Holiday worshippers crowding the large hall would be able to see me. The memories transported me to a world so beautiful, yet so far removed from the brutal reality. How could that transformation have happened in just a few short years?

Cantor Sherman's passionate plea on Yom Kippur: "Do not abandon us; do not remove your holy spirit from us" jolted my mind with pain. God did abandon my family and my people.

"Being bitter will not help us now, Mehal," Joseph consoled me, when I shared my thoughts with him. "We have to go on; we have to fight for a better world, despite the catastrophe."

"I feel that all our prayers to an Almighty God have been in vain, and our belief in a God who turned out to be blind to this catastrophe, was a farce," I answered Joseph, on our way back to my uncle's house.

"Mehal, Mehal," Joseph said. "You certainly said a mouthful, but it is not quite correct. You see, you're taking the words of the prayers too literally. God is certainly not a king, not a general. He doesn't have any mechanized armies to fight evil men like Hitler. God is an idea, a concept, not a corporal being."

His words startled me: "What do you mean by an idea, a concept?" I asked.

"God as an idea is the embodiment of perfection: perfection of justice, fairness, compassion, goodness and peace. It's the ultimate standard of human behavior, in resonance with the harmony in the universe," Joseph answered.

"And what do you do with this idea?" I asked.

169

"You try to strive for it. You try to make others strive for it. You make people—all people—agree to achieve those ultimate standards and then, only then, will you be able to avoid the likes of Hitler," Joseph said.

"And meanwhile, how would you prevent violence and crimes?" I sharply asked.

"We Jews talk about the Messianic era. We have no date for it, and the belief that the Messiah will arrive on a white horse one day is also a myth. I rather think that each day that we do some good, each day that we live in peace, we advance the coming of the Messiah, and we advance the concept of God as an idea."

I admired Joseph's lofty language, which, however, did not quiet the turmoil within me, the anger at the whole world and God for the murder of my people.

Rivka introduced us to several survivors of the ghetto and the executions. One of them, Reuben Cantor, offered to go with us to the mass graves of the last "action," where some 5,000 Jews, including Reuben's parents, Joseph's parents, and my parents and relatives— the remainder of the ghetto—were murdered on October 5, 1942. The early, sunny November day turned drizzly in the after-noon. As we walked, Reuben described the scene of the executions which he, wounded, miraculously managed to survive.

German soldiers, but mostly Ukrainian Gendarmes, lined the Jews up in groups of several dozen, at the edge of the ditch that previously had been dug up in the ravine next to the Ikva River. A young German, chain-smoking cigarettes, kept firing his machine gun at the victims, most of whom were still alive when the Gendarmes pushed them, one on top of the other, into the ditch.

Reuben, wounded in the shoulder, freed himself from the dying bodies at night, picked up some clothes, and fled into the outlying forests. There he joined other partisans who harassed the German supply lines, putting wooden logs and other heavy objects on railroad tracks to derail trains, so they could steal the goods and arms that they carried.

When we reached the ravine, we saw a young boy shepherding a few cows grazing in the lush field. Reuben pointed to the bones and skulls scattered for several hundred meters and explained that there were layers and layers of martyrs in the ground underneath. "You see this corner here? That's where I was able to get hold of some rocks and crawl out from the grave," Reuben said.

The little boy stopped by and looked at us.

"Whose bones are these?" I asked him.

"They are bones of wild animals," he said, and went off.

We stood there, shocked into silence. The pastoral scene, contrasting with the heinous crime, jarred my mind. The bucolic quietude clashed with shrieks of men, women, and children being led to their slaughter, which it seemed I heard from the depth of the pit. I felt dizzy and disoriented. I could not reconcile my being alive with the deaths of my parents, the deaths of so many, the death of my whole town. I shivered, angry and cold. I pictured being there in the pit with my parents, grandmother, aunt, and little Henry—being with them all. I felt a bullet piercing my heart and warm blood spilling over my body. Then I pictured shovels of earth, heavy earth over me, sinking me down into the abyss. I was dying, but Mother and Father were there with me. I felt nausea rise up to my throat, filling my mouth, as we said *Kaddish* and left.

On the way back to Uncle's house, I remembered a heartrending prayer the famed Cantor Jacob Kussevitzki chanted in a concert he gave in the Great Synagogue before the War. "*Havet Meeshomayim Ur'ay...*" Look from heaven and see...that we have been derided among the nations; we have been led like sheep to slaughter...." The prayer dated to the 12th century, when the Crusaders slaughtered Jews throughout western Europe on their way to worship Christ in Jerusalem. The plague of Jew-hatred lives on, virulent and terrifying, as of old, I thought.

"Why didn't the Jews fight back?" I asked Reuben.

"Because we lost our will to live and all hope of surviving, even if we could run away," Reuben said. He explained that running away would have jeopardized the lives of everyone else in the ghetto. For example, one day the number of people returning from a work assignment did not match the number that had left in the morning; the next day, the Germans hanged ten men, picked at random, as punishment.

"The ghetto became a prison, ruled by vicious armed beasts, and surrounded by vultures, the Ukrainians, who stole Jewish property and homes, and eagerly helped the Germans in their grisly tasks. Towards the end, we knew we would all die but could do nothing about it," he concluded.

"You should visit the place," I said to Luba and Moniek when we returned to Uncle's house. I described to them the scene Joe and I had witnessed, accompanied by Reuben, and told them about his escape from the mass grave and his survival in the woods. "I am sick; this has been the worst day of my life!" I exclaimed, as my voice broke in anger.

"Mehal, you had no business going there!" Luba yelled.

"What do you mean?!" I shouted back.

"Stop acting like a big shot, carrying all the world's burdens."

"Luba, don't talk down to me. Don't dismiss me as if I was a kid."

"You should thank God we are alive," Moniek interjected.

"Should I also thank God for letting His people be slaughtered?" I answered.

172

"It is an offense to question's God's ways!" Moniek raised his voice.

"A God who witnessed this catastrophe and had no power to stop it does not deserve my respect," I exclaimed and left the room.

The encounter left me shaken. Luba and Moniek had no regard for me and my feelings; they were together now and treated me as if I were of no consequence to them. I had begun to feel estranged from them on the day they married in Lvov, and this exchange confirmed my feelings. Suddenly, I felt even more alone and much older, indeed, as old as my people, abandoned and wounded.

That night, I dreamed my parents were next to me, and beyond them were thousands of skeletons. I narrowed my sight on my parents and saw them as I had so many times since I had seen the wounded, dying soldier in Shepetovka. Father had his throat slashed open, with blood pulsating from his wounds. Mother lay on Father's right side, leaning peacefully against his shoulder, pale, almost white. Father, looking straight at me with open eyes, lay so close to me I actually touched him and caressed his hair.

"Tatte," I said, "Luba and I have come home, but there is no one here. They are all in mass graves. Are you and Mother there? You told me people were good. You taught me to have faith. But no one cared—not even God—to stop the killings."

Then Father spoke. "The earth has turned into *Tohu Vavohu*, waste and wilderness, and an evil darkness is sweeping over its abyss."

"Tatte, I want to stay with you and Mother," I said.

"Go," he whispered and closed his lids.

"Tatte, I love you," I cried, but he did not answer. I heard Mother whisper, "I love you, Mehal," and I woke up, drenched with sweat.

Filled with remorse, I whispered, "I should have been with Father, I should have been with Mother. I should have never left them." I felt so guilty, so ashamed of letting them down. Who was I to survive while so many, nearly everybody, perished?

My visit to the mass graves convinced me we could no longer stay in Dubno, and, reconciled, I agreed with Luba and Moniek that it was time to leave.

Luba had lost no time searching for a buyer of our home and that of Grandmother. To my great surprise, she found a Russian businessman interested in the properties, who paid 250 U.S. dollars for each house, an unbelievable sum of money for us.

"Now we have enough to buy our way through the borders and into West Germany," Luba exclaimed gleefully, showing me the crisp U.S. $50 bills.

"What about the Ukrainian who lives there now?" I asked.

"The Ukrainian lives there illegally and the buyer will evict him in no time; he's pretty well-connected with the town hall people," Luba said.

The next day, Moniek, Luba, and I decided to leave and join Moniek's mother and relatives in Krakow. I bid goodbye to Joseph, who had to stay to reclaim his property.

The next morning, Luba, Moniek and I headed to the train station. Our route took us through Lvov again, followed by a train trip to Krakow. Krakow had the oldest Jewish community in Poland. It dated to the 14th century when Kazimiesz the Great had invited Jewish merchants to help build his commerce. Through the centuries Krakow had become a thriving, vibrant Jewish community of close to 100,000 Jews.

We rushed to see Moniek's mother upon our arrival to Krakow, and were pleasantly surprised to find Joseph and Leena there as well. Moniek's mother, Eva Perlman, a tall, stately woman with gray hair, a wrinkled, angular face, broad lips, and bright, blue eyes, displayed much energy and vitality. She lit up as she embraced Moniek.

"What a miracle it is to see you all here," she exclaimed. "After so much tragedy, it's wonderful to see my boys, well, and married too. I can't believe my own eyes, but it's true, thank God. If only your father were here. I have so much to tell you," she said, choking with emotion, and left the room.

She came back later, asked us to wash up, and invited us to the kitchen, where she served us some food. "It is an unbelievable story, but miracles did happen, even during this dreadful period," she said, as she told us of the demise of the Krakow Jews. Shortly after entering Krakow in the fall of 1939, the Germans began to harass the Jews. They picked people at random and beat them or hanged them in public. They deprived the Jews of food, seized Jewish property at will, and made life unbearable. In the fall of 1940, they set up a ghetto and crowded all the Jews into a small area of the city. A few months later, they began to transfer thousands of Jews to a nearby concentration camp at Plaszow.

Oscar Schindler, a German contractor who supplied strategic goods for the German army and had many connections with top German authorities in Krakow, decided to recruit Jewish people, destined for the concentration camp, for work in his factories. Moniek's cousin, Regina, was among the first that Schindler employed as his secretary. She succeeded in convincing Schindler to select Moniek's mother, his uncles, and a few of the cousins to work for him. Schindler saved about 3,000 Jews that way, a good part of Moniek's family among them.

"And what happened to Father?" Moniek asked.

"The Germans had taken your father and other men out to work in a factory twenty or so miles away from Krakow before

Schindler came into the picture. From there, he was sent to another factory, then became ill and died," Moniek's mother answered.

As the conversation went on, it became clear that the Jews of Krakow had suffered the same fate as the Jews of Lvov and Dubno—almost all of them were killed.

Moniek's mother set up one of the bedrooms of her small apartment for the three of us to stay.

The next day, we met Regina Wolf, the cousin who had saved nearly half the Perlman family while working as a secretary for Schindler. A tall, vivacious woman in her 30s, she exuded confidence and cheer. Easy to speak with, she filled in details about Oscar Schindler, whom she described as a temperamental and often drunk egotist, who, nevertheless, became obsessed with saving Jews destined for the gas chambers.

Later in the day, another of Moniek's cousins, Naftali Eckstein, visited us. He had spent several years in the Mathausen concentration camp, where he nearly perished from starvation and illness. Naftali, now a stout man in his 40s, with a round face and mischievous eyes, purveyed good humor and funny stories. He had been engaged in a mission to help Jews returning from the concentration camps and the Soviet Union to leave for Germany.

The Poles had no use for the survivors of the catastrophe; like the Ukrainians in the East, they had appropriated Jewish property, and they were determined to hold onto it. Meanwhile, West Germany, particularly the part occupied by the United States, had "porous borders" and provided refuge for the Jewish survivors. The Joint Distribution Committee sponsored efforts to help the survivors escape from Poland to Germany, and Naftali had been engaged to facilitate that task.

Soon after our arrival, Naftali arranged for us to leave Krakow through Czechoslovakia. Towards the end of December, Moniek's mother, Joseph, Leena, Moniek, Luba, and I crossed the Polish-Czech border at Szchechin. From there, we took a train to Prague, where we stayed a few days. On Christmas Eve 1945, we went to a small, border town across the river from Hoff, Germany. Naftali's friends explained to us that Christmas Eve would be a good time to cross the river, since most of the border guards would be celebrating the holiday with their families. The friends also arranged for guides to carry us across the shallow waters of the river.

At midnight Christmas morning, we arrived in the U.S. Occupation Zone in West Germany, and later that day traveled by train to Munich. Finally, and ironically, we felt free and secure, in the murderers' den, the city that had incubated the Nazi plague. We made our way to the United Nations Relief and Rehabilitation Agency (UNRRA), which assigned us to live in the displaced persons' camp at Landsberg, the town famous for its jail, where Hitler had written, in the 1920s, *Mein Kampf,* his manifesto for exterminating the Jews. I felt queasy about it and mentioned it to Luba. "Don't worry," she said, "it is only a halfway place to all sorts of destinations, and a new beginning."

"You are a great optimist, my wonderful Lubushka, Galubushka," I said as we embraced.

Judenrein

No Monuments to the Fallen

There are no monuments to the fallen, in Dubno,
Nor in any shtetl of Belarus and Ukraine.
But come and see, in the pastoral fields near Dubno,
Skulls and limbs scattered in a ravine.
There are no traces of slaughter in Dubno,
No ovens, no showers, no remains of deadly gas.
But come and learn: along the Ikva River,
The Germans shot and buried young and old en masse.
Shrapnelled shards of a shattered past
Sear my soul and pierce my mind.
Alas! I write these lines at life's dusk
Our dead to honor as well as wounds to bind.
And, also, to add wings to my humble prayer that
This tribe from Sarah and Abraham begotten,
Its teachings, its culture, with pain and courage bred,
Shall not perish, nor be forgotten!

By Michael G. Kesler

Letters to Tatte (Father)

Landsberg DP Camp – August 1946

Tatte, I need to talk to you. I miss you and Momme very much. I feel alone. When I came here in January, with Luba and her husband, Moniek, I became ill and stayed in the hospital a long time. The doctor told me that I injured my heart muscles, due to stress. Grief, following my visit to the mass graves to see where you and Momme had been buried, took a toll on me. I felt guilty that I had left you, fleeing with Luba.

Soon after leaving the hospital, I joined a *kibbutz* to train as a farmer for going to Palestine. We stayed up late last night, ready to board buses for Hamburg, where a ship would be waiting to take us there. But the buses never came. Our leaders told us that the British had intercepted and diverted the ship to Cyprus; they don't want us Jews in Palestine. No other country wants us either. Am I to spend the rest of my life in barracks of a displaced persons' camp?! Tatte, I hurt; I'm full of anger!

Tatte, I remember our return to Dubno after you had been fired as a forester by Graf Zamoyski, because of being Jewish. I recall how desperately you tried to emigrate with the family to Palestine, but the British restricted Jewish influx to the Promised Land. Twelve years and six million deaths later, your son faces the same monster you faced: the plague of anti-Semitism that devours the world's decency and sanity. The enclosed sketch and poem illustrate my state of mind.

Where Shall I Go?

Where shall I go with all the gates shut?
Where shall I go with all exit roads cut?
Can you hear my fervent plea?
This poison place I must flee,
But wherever I'd go, they'd trample on me!
Can you see? Can't you see?

(A Yiddish Song of the Post-War Era)

Change of Fortune – November 1946

Tatte, an UNRRA official, a Jewish colonel, has just handed me a letter from Colby College in Waterville, Maine, with unbelievable news that I have been accepted as a student for the fall 1947 semester! Two months earlier, I had enrolled at the *München Technische Hochshule* to study engineering. One day, I came across a notice from B'nai Brith Hillel about U.S. scholarships being offered to deserving displaced persons of student age, and I applied. Yesterday's news that I have won the scholarship filled me with a joy I have not known since before leaving home. Can you imagine your son going to America and maybe becoming an engineer some day?

Another sweet surprise: Luba has given birth to a boy! Tatte, we're so jubilant! So happy! What a thrill to hold the little baby in my arms! He quickens my pulse; he makes me giggle and laugh; I feel like dancing; I feel like bursting with happiness. Luba is doing well, and she'll return to the barracks soon.

Tatte, Luba has contacted Momme's sister, Leah, in Uruguay. She and Moniek are preparing to emigrate to that country, one of the very few that accept Jewish survivors. I will be leaving soon for America. Pray for me. I am so excited, hoping that I will find a new life there.

Healing in Paris – Spring 1947

Tatte, I have made a pleasant detour on the way to America. HIAS (Hebrew Immigration Aid Society) officials had arranged that I establish residence in Paris before I apply to emigrate, since the United States stopped issuing visas to displaced persons in Germany. While here, I work as a radio technician, having learned the vocation in the displaced persons' camp. This sojourn, hopefully brief, has filled me with joy, as it has opened for me a new world of beauty, well-being, and excitement. In fact, I have renewed my habit of writing poetry, and the one below conveys, better than prose, my excitement of being here.

Healing
I fell in love, as if in a trance,
with the city of wonder, the city of lights,
Paris, the beauty, the jewel of France,
and its audacious embrace of time and space.
My soul sprung to life as if released from a sling,
and explored with delight its gardens and parks,
the Notre Dame, the Sacre Coeur and the heights of Montmartre,
and the Louvre exploding with a kaleidoscope of art.
My soul found healing in the concert halls,
in tune with Eroica and Elixir of Love,
in resonance with lovers' embrace,
amidst gentle cooing of doves.
My soul found peace with a prayer shawl,
a choir chant that I sang as a child,
remembering the past with a dear friend,
challenging God and the premise of Faith.
These events and more mended my soul
and I began to feel whole.

A New Kesler in the Family – November 1953

Tatte, you have a new grandson! My lovely Regina has given birth to our first son, whom we are going to name after you, Moshe (Mark). I think he looks like you, too: he has your brown hair, large green eyes, and broad lips. He smiles when I tickle him. He holds my finger firmly in his grip. He listens carefully when I sing to him. He is a delight to hold and sway to-and-fro. He makes me so excited. I want to live and prosper and have more children as cute as he....

I wish you and Momme were here to see your little grandson and meet his wonderful mother. Regina and her family had fled Suwalki, Poland, in 1939, lived in Vilna for a year or so and, deported to a Siberian slave-labor camp and subsequently released, spent the war in Kyrgyzstan. At war's end, Regina and her family had emigrated to Sweden, and in 1947, Regina had come to the United States and later entered and completed Harvard Medical School.

Tatte, Regina is a dynamo, born to be a physician; she loves children and loves life. She is warm and kind, and I feel blessed that I have found her!

We met a few years ago, while I was finishing my chemical engineering studies at M.I.T., the world's finest engineering school! I had studied with renowned professors who opened exciting wonders of technology for me and most of all, taught me to think freely and firmly, and boldly to challenge accepted convention. I am now working as a researcher for one of my professors, my mentor, and I am filled with pride and hope. Did you or Momme ever think your son would be a chemical engineer?!

Tatte, Luba and I are together again! I have been able to bring her, her husband, Moniek, their son, Nathan, six, and his one-year-old sister, Manya, to the United States from Uruguay. They will be living in New York City. Moniek is a gifted inventor and has had no difficulty finding work as a mechanic.

The Family is Growing....Fall 1959

Tatte, Regina has just given birth to our third child, whom we named David, after her uncle who just passed away. He is plump and cuddly, and Mark, now six and his sister, May, four, love to play with him, although they are both a bit jealous. I wish I would have more time to hold him and play with him, but getting settled in our new home keeps me too busy.

Oh yes! Last year, we moved into this beautiful home, our first. I helped design it, and it includes spacious living quarters and Regina's offices. Regina loves her new facilities, as well as her growing number of young patients. Her energy knows no bounds, nor do her good humor and cheer.

We live in Paramus, New Jersey, a town of some 30,000 people, a lovely suburb of New York City. The sizable and growing Jewish community has welcomed us warmly and, in fact, has asked me to be their synagogue cantor. My years of studying with Cantor Sherman in Dubno have not been in vain, Tatte. I enjoy so much being able to give of my inner self and knowing that I serve the needs of a large community of my people. Music means so much to me: when I sing, I am as if transported to another world; I feel a sweetness sweep through my body, filling me with a happiness I can hardly contain. The prayers of the High Holidays, full of passion and pathos, bring me so close to you and Momme, as I remember how proud you were of my chanting as a soprano soloist in the Great Synagogue choir.

Tatte, I feel I'm bursting with desire to do well. I just presented a paper, the first of its kind, on using computers, very fast calculators, and memory-storage devices to help engineers design petroleum-refining equipment. The paper generated tremendous interest at the conference. I believe this paper will open up wonderful opportunities for me.

Recovering from the Tragic Loss of Regina – Fall of 1978

Tatte, Regina has died! I still feel devastated, even though it happened five years ago. She had become ill with cancer five years earlier and struggled bravely to live on, but after years of treatment and pain and suffering, she succumbed to the disease. She left me bereft, as if I had lost all my limbs. I thought I would lose my mind from grief and loneliness, and yet….

Regina left me with four precious kids, with Ted (12), born since my last letter to you. Her death has shocked them all. She had showered much love on them; filled the home with laughter and joy, as well as attended to the daily necessities of growing children. She has left a terrible void, which I, poorly equipped, have tried to fill these last few years.

Acting both as mother and father has put a heavy load on me. MIT had not offered any courses on how to meet the needs of talented, but not very disciplined, teenagers. No extended-family members have come to my rescue…. I searched alone through the maze of pathways to understand my children, born and raised in a different country, set on a fast track of changing mores and customs. Things are nearly stable now, though I still feel lonely and restless.

Your niece, Eeta, and her husband, Gershon – who had survived the war in the Soviet Union and settled in Israel a few years

187

after the war – invited me to visit them. Eeta wanted to introduce me to a woman, a close friend of the family; she promised a great surprise when I arrive. She met me at the airport in Tel Aviv with her brother, Hershl, at her side. I was stunned! I hadn't seen Hershl from the day the NKVD snatched him away in Voroshilovograd in the summer of 1941!

I soon learned that, after taking Hershl into custody and learning that he was completely deaf, the NKVD handed him over to the military, who sent him to a camp supporting the troops, where he became the warehouse manager. Two truck drivers attempted to steal some food, and when Hershl intervened to stop them, they turned against him. At Christmastime, the drivers, drunk, knocked out the camp's generator with their truck. Apprehended, they claimed that Hershl directed them to do it. The NKVD arrested Hershl and tortured him for months, forcing him to confess his alleged crime. The confession sealed his exile to northern Siberia, where he nearly perished from hunger, cold, and hard labor. Released in 1957, he made his way to Israel, with the help of Eeta and Gershon. Married, he is doing well and lives with his wife's family in Tel Aviv. I shivered as I listened to Hershl's account. I felt fortunate that Luba and I had been able to leave the Soviet Union.

The hustle and bustle of Tel Aviv startled and thrilled me. Cranes loomed at nearly every corner, and the din of construction filled the streets. The miraculous rebirth of the country, where you and I had dreamed of living, filled me with pride and exhilaration. Tatte, I wish you were here to see what our brethren have achieved in the 30 years since David Ben Gurion proclaimed Israel's independence in May 1948. I returned home alone, but the visit filled me with inspiration and increased my drive to do well.

Tatte, I feel elated with the progress I have made in my profession, despite the personal difficulties. Having obtained a doctorate in chemical engineering from a prestigious university, I have in the last few years published a number of important papers to help engineers design oil-refinery plants better and much faster. My name—your name—is becoming well-known throughout the industry. I feel so happy to be productive, to be needed, to be helpful; it mitigates the sting of Regina's loss.

I should tell you, Tatte, that Moniek and Luba have been doing extremely well since coming here. Moniek developed machines to automate zipper production and has been marketing these wonder machines all over the world.

Married Again – October 1985

Tatte, I'm so happy to tell you that I have married a wonderful woman named Barbara. She reminds me of Momme, being short, having black hair, dark eyes, and the same lively disposition. She is bold and smart; she teaches journalism at the university here. She brings a 16-year-old boy, Michael, and a 12-year-old girl, Esther, to the family, lovely children that I am very fond of. We have moved to a new home, which we are busy fitting to the needs of both families. I feel happy again.

Six years ago, I founded my own firm, offering consulting to improve oil-refining operations. The two oil companies, the largest in the world, where I had spent most of my career, treated me well. Yet I have always felt an outsider, with subtle limits in the ladder I could climb. More than that, I often felt like a little cog in a huge wheel, linked to an infinite network of other wheels that squashed my initiative, and left me restless and frustrated. In any event, since my days at MIT, I have been driven to pursue my own dreams and do my own thing.

The last few years have made me mature professionally and personally; I feel I have become more self-reliant and confident, as well as more competent. I have also done well, easing the burden of financing the children's education, as well as providing for a more comfortable and interesting lifestyle.

Going Blind –Fall of 2009

Tatte, 25 years ago I began to lose my eyesight due to an illness called glaucoma. By the way, Luba, as well as Hershl who died several years ago at 95, have suffered from the same disease. In the last three years, I have turned nearly blind, and the world around me grows dark. Indeed, not being able to do or direct the work, I sold my consulting business. I have since rewritten and published Regina's memoir—which she wrote in the last years of her life, and have been busy writing about my own past.

Many years have gone by since I last wrote to you, and they brought many happy events. All our six children are married and have families of their own. Barbara and I have 11 grandchildren, six of whom are your great-grandchildren! We try to meet with all of them several times a year, though they are scattered around the country. Our children and their spouses form an extraordinary assembly of professionals, including engineers, an architect, a psychologist, four educators, a physical therapist, and—believe it or not—two rabbis!

I wish so much that you and Momme could witness your little great-grandchildren at play or the noisy discussions at family gatherings. Tatte, it should cheer you to no end to learn that Luba and Moniek have three children, 12 grandchildren, and 17 great-grandchildren!

Tatte, I now have more time to think and wonder about my past and the present. My eyes fill with tears when I think of the primordial evil that extinguished the lives of six million of our people, including yours and Momme's. I find the contrast between my children's lives and my early life in the land of hatred and violence preceding the catastrophe bewildering. Tatte, we live in a great, beautiful, and unique country, blessed with good weather, riches of the soil and its waters and, most important, with good people who have come from all over the world. I wish you were here to see Ukrainians living next door to Jews, their children mingling and inter-marrying, and their grandchildren playing and learning to be good to one another. There are more languages spoken here than in the Tower of Babel, yet the people talk freely and understand one another—and a black man leads them all! No, the streets of New York City are not paved with gold, but they are filled often with multitudes from scores of nations joining for each other's celebrations—and a Jewish mayor presides over this magnificent city! I feel that I, our children, and grandchildren— your great-grandchildren—are secure here. And yet....

Ill winds of hatred and violence, jealousy and envy are whip-sawing the world around us. Religious leaders teach tens of millions of children to hate and turn tens of thousands into human missiles to kill and maim endless numbers of innocents in the name of their Almighty God. Vitriol and venom are their language, full of lies and malice. And—you guessed it—the Jew is their target, again! It hurts, Tatte, it hurts!

Rest in peace, Tatte, wherever you are. I wish I could tell Momme that her parting words, "I love you, Mehal," still ring in my ears; they have served me well through the years. I love you both and miss you very much.

The Rise and Demise of Jewish Life in Ukraine

Dubno, my hometown in the province of Volyn, now Ukraine, had been ruled through the centuries by various masters as, indeed, was the fate of much of Ukraine. The Russians ruled Ukraine for over a century, until the end of World War I. In 1920, Poland became the master of the western part of Ukraine, including Volyn, as dictated by the Treaty of Versailles. In September 1939, with the outbreak of World War II, the Russians re-occupied Volyn as part of the eastern half of Poland.

The following pages are intended to clarify the history of the region of my birth. It also provides an overview of Jewish history in Ukraine, as well as of their annihilation, as background for the events described in the main body of the book.

A. Jews in Ukraine

According to Henry Abramson, archaeological evidence places early Jewish settlement in Ukraine in antiquity, possibly several centuries BCE (Before the Common Era) with the Greek colonization of the Black Sea coast.[1] Little is known about the Jews' presence in this area until its conquest by the Khazars, a semi-nomadic people from Central Asia, who had founded their kingdom near the Caspian Sea and the Caucasus, including eastern Ukraine, southern Russia, and Crimea. Faced with the emerging power of the Muslims to the south and the Christians to the west, the Khazar leadership decided to adopt a competing monotheistic religion; in 740, they converted *en masse* to Judaism. The Jewish Khazars' influence on the Slavic entity continued as evidenced by the presence of Jewish quarters in Kiev in the 11th century.

The extraordinary story of the conversion of the Khazars to Judaism had attracted the attention of the 12th-century Jewish scholar, Yehuda Halevi of Spain,[2] as well as of the 20th-century Hungarian writer, Arthur Koestler.[3] The story fascinates me personally, since my father and many of his family looked very much like Ukrainians, with a stocky frame, brown-reddish hair and light green eyes. Indeed, a goodly portion of the Jews of my hometown had similar traits, distinctly different from the typical Semitic ones.

The Khazar empire went on the decline in the following two centuries, due to the establishment of a Slavic Ukraine, Kievan Rus, in 882. In the 11th century, Kievan Rus became geographically the largest state in Europe, becoming known in the rest of Europe as Ruthenia. Subsequent power struggles between the various municipalities and onslaughts by nomadic people from the East undermined Kievan Rus's integrity. In the 12th and 13th

[1] Abramson, Henry, *A Prayer for the Government,* Massachusetts, Harvard University Press, 1999, p. 1.
[2] Halevi, Yehuda, *The Kuzari,* Spain, Jason Aronson, Inc, 1998.
[3] Koestler, Arthur, *The Thirteenth Tribe,* New York: Random House, 1976.

centuries, Kievan Rus became prey to invading Mongols from Central Asia. During the next few hundred years, the Lithuanian kingdom began to dominate the area, and had consolidated its rule when, in 1569, it merged with Poland to form the Polish-Lithuanian Commonwealth. The commonwealth's dominance opened the vast, fertile area to massive immigration from Poland, and an accompanying influx of western culture and Catholicism. The ensuing cultural and religious clash between the newcomers and the native population gave rise to the formation of the Don Cossacks, ferocious horsemen, who became an unruly militant power over much of Ukraine.

These events marked the beginning of a mass migration of Jews into Ukraine. Large numbers of Jews had begun to settle in Poland towards the end of the 14th century at the invitation of King Casmir the Great. During the following two centuries, the Jews established themselves as merchants, artisans, money-lenders, and servants of the Polish nobility.

The Polish conquest of Ukraine provided great opportunities for the Jews to help the Polish nobility settle and develop the possession. The Polish aristocrats, preferring the conviviality in Warsaw—and often Paris—to the drudgery of farming or com-merce, offered tempting opportunities for Jews. The Jews became the tax collectors, the tavern owners, the merchants in the growing cities, and, in many instances, town/village administra-tors. They also became the primary targets of the rising ire of the impoverished serfs and particularly the Cossacks. In the 1648 uprising, the Cossacks, led by Bohdan Khmelnytski, swept through Ukraine, destroying nearly a third of the Jewish popula-tion, presaging the pogroms and the Holocaust of later centuries. Yet the Jews persevered and slowly rebuilt their communities.

Significantly, the Khmelnystski devastation robbed the Jews of their ability to maintain traditional Jewish life, based on scholarly pursuit of the Torah and the Talmud. A new form of observance, known as Chasidism, came to life and emphasized song and dance as a way to heal and bind the communities. This movement flourished throughout Ukraine and Poland for the following several centuries.

With the partition and disappearance of Poland in 1797, most of Ukraine came under the rule of Russia, which designated the area as one of the major "pales of settlement," where the Jews were permitted to live and, indeed, spread their economic and cultural dominance. During the 19th century, and until the Soviet Revolution in 1917, the Jewish population had grown and had become the largest in the world at the turn of the 20th century. Its scholars, poets, and political leaders took up the banners of the *Haskalah* (Enlightenment) sweeping through Europe as well as through Zionism and socialism.

The 19th century saw a dramatic population shift in Ukraine, with about 85 percent of Jews moving into the large cities, where they often constituted up to one-half or more of the inhabitants. The Jews acquired major (and often controlling) interests in trade, particularly foreign trade, and in manufacturing, commerce, and business. They dominated the professions, the arts, and Ukraine's cultural life. Yiddish, the language spoken by 98 percent of Ukrainian Jews, became the *lingua franca* of the Jews throughout Europe and in the Americas. In a seminal lecture, "The Rise and Fall of the Yiddish Empire," delivered on March 13, 2008, at the Yivo Institute in New York City, Benjamin Harshav, professor of comparative literature at Yale University, painted a panoramic picture of the great cultural, commercial, financial, and political influence of the Yiddish-speaking Jews, particularly of Ukraine.

At the turn of the 20th century, it appeared that the Jews had achieved near dominance in the urban world of Ukraine, except for lack of their defense around the islands of their relative prosperity. This lack of effective means to defend themselves from the seething hostility of the world surrounding the towns and cities where they had lived and prospered exposed the Jews to existential dangers and ultimate ruin.

About 85 percent of Ukrainians remained on the farms, most often as serfs, until their liberation in the mid-1800s. While the Jews had expanded economically and culturally, the lives of the peasants remained harsh, even after their emancipation. As the wave of nationalism spread through the West, Ukrainians' drive for independence intensified, as did their leaders' scapegoating of Jews for their economic malaise. Political unrest, as well as the contrasting lifestyles and culture of Jews, intensified Ukrainians' hostility and resulted in violent pogroms against Jews in the second half of the 19th century. This gave rise to a large wave of Jewish immigration to the United States. Indeed, about 80 percent of American Jewry in the pre-World War II era could trace their origin to Ukraine.

The 1917 revolution in Russia gave rise to open warfare between the Ukrainians, fighting for independence under the leadership of Simon Petlura, the Bolsheviks ascending in power in Russia, and the White Russians, under General Denikin, opposing the Bolsheviks as well as the Ukrainians. The cauldron of conflict caught the Jews in the middle and led to their loss of 150,000 of their people and to the devastation of many of their communities, on the hands of Petlura's, as well Denikin's forces.[4]

---

[4] Midlarsky, Manus, *The Killing Trap,* New York, Cambridge University Press, 2005, p. 45.

In 1917, after the Russian Revolution, Ukraine underwent cataclysmic upheavals that included the formation of an independent government. After a very short period of cooperation with the Jews, the Ukrainians, under the leadership of Simon Petlura, turned violently against the Jews, blaming them as the agents of Bolshevism that stood in the way of Ukraine becoming independent. During the next two years, Petlura and his followers swept through Ukraine, in the footsteps of the 17th-century Khmelnystski, and massacred tens of thousands of Jews.

The Versailles Treaty, which sealed the new postwar borders in Europe, handed the western part of Ukraine to Poland, with the eastern part becoming the Ukrainian Soviet Socialist Republic (Ukrainian SSR), a part of the Soviet Union. In the next two decades which preceded World War II, both the western Ukraine under Poland and the eastern, as part of the Soviet Union, seethed with unrest.

The Ukrainian Soviet Socialist Republic (SSR) witnessed significant industrialization and migration from the farms to the cities, largely as a result of forcible, often violent collectivization of farms and dispersal of well-to-do farmers (Kulaks) to far-flung corners of the Soviet Union. The collectivization created economic and social havoc, and increased Ukrainians' hostility towards the Soviet regime and Communist implementers and administrators of the new policies. Significantly, the administrators were often Communists (Bolsheviks) of Jewish origin.

In the western Ukraine, the nationalistic fervor, frustrated by the defeat and exile of Petlura and his subsequent 1926 assassination by a Jew in Paris, gave rise to the Ukrainians' drive for independence from the Poles, as well as to mounting hatred of the Jews.

The 20s saw the formation of a fascist Ukrainian party, Ukrainian Military Organization (UVO), that collaborated in the late 30s with the Nazi regime.[5] With the approach of World War II and the growth of the Nazi shadow over Europe, the Ukrainians increasingly saw their hopes for independence tied to Hitler's objective of defeating Bolshevism. When Hitler's armies marched into the Soviet Union on June 22, 1941, the Ukrainians became the Germans' most enthusiastic allies and most eager collaborators.

B. The Aftermath

[*The events described in this section pertain to Ukraine at its current borders, set when it became an independent country in 1992.*] Before Hitler's invasion of the Soviet Union in June 1941, this area had the largest Jewish population in Europe, second only to that of the United States. Kruglov puts that population at 2.7 million.[6] Providing a tabulation and analysis of the killings in each *oblast* (region), Kruglov concludes that the Germans, with the help of the local population, killed 1.6 million Jews in Ukraine between 1941 and 1943.[7] This tally is consistent with numbers quoted by Joshua Rubenstein[8] and Boris Zabarko[9].

Nearly half of the Jews of the Ukrainian Soviet Republic survived; indeed, the Soviet Union evacuated many as essential workers of the factories, industries, and institutions. In the

---

[5] Sabrin, B.F., *Alliance for Murder,* New York: Sarpedon, 1991, p. 4.
[6] Brandon, Ray and Lower, Wendy, eds. *The Shoah in Ukraine*. Bloomington, Indiana: Indiana University Press, 2008, Chapter 8, p. 273.
[7] *Ibid*
[8] Rubenstein, Joshua; Altman, Ilya, eds. *The Unknown Black Book*. Bloomington, Indiana: Indiana University Press, 2008, p. xvii.
[9] Zabarko, Boris, ed. *Holocaust in the Ukraine*. Oregon: Vallentine Mitchell, 2005, p. xiii.

Western Ukraine, the first week of Hitler's offensive against the Soviets on June 22, 1941, proved disastrous for the Soviets and fatal for the Jews who had been swallowed up by the German war and hate machine. Dieter Pohl cites that a total of about 40,000 – 50,000 Jews, out of a total of approximately 1,000,000 fled that area to the Soviet Union.[10] Very few Jews who had remained behind survived the mass killings and executions that followed.

About 240,000 Jews had left the German-occupied western part of Poland within months of the fall of Poland on September 17, 1939.[11] These refugees settled temporarily in the Western Ukraine, as well as in Belarus and Lithuania, until Stalin's secret police apprehended most of the refugees and scattered them throughout the vastness of Siberia. Luckily, the overwhelming majority of these refugees managed to survive, often against terrible odds.

Related statistics include the number and percentage of Polish Jews who survived the Holocaust; Lucy Dawidowicz estimates that number to be 300,000, or approximately 10 percent[12]. The overwhelming amount of the 300,000 survived the war by fleeing to, or through, the Soviet Union and then returning to Poland after the war. The Jews who survived the war in Poland proper, or in various concentration camps outside Poland, numbered about 50,000, or less than two percent of the total prewar Jewish population. (Polish Jews refers to Jews who lived in the pre-World

---

[10] Brandon, Ray and Lower, Wendy et al, Op. cited, p. 25.
[11] Davies, Norman, Polonsky, Antony, ed. *Jews in Eastern Poland and the USSR, 1939-46.* New York: St. Martin's Press, 1991, p. 113.
[12] Dawidowicz, Lucy, *The War Against the Jews, 1933-1945.* New York: Holt, Rinehart and Winston, 1975, p. 403.

War II borders of Poland.) After this annexation of the eastern half of Poland by the Soviet Union on September 17, 1939, about one-half of the so-called Polish Jews came under Soviet domination.

The annihilation of the Jews of Ukraine differed in significant detail and preceded, by over a year, the extermination of the Jews of Poland, and Central and Western Europe. The Germans organized the latter on an industrialized scale with sophisticated automation, requiring relatively few people in the killing process. This included the transport of victims by rail to distant "work" camps, ending with their deaths in gas chambers and crematoria. By contrast, most of the killings of the Jews in Ukraine required enormously larger direct intervention by individuals.

However, Ukraine was not devoid of concentration camps and other automated, mass-murder facilities. The Janowska labor/death camp near Lvov claimed the lives of several hundred-thousand Jews, with the majority of the victims coming from outside Ukraine.[13] Ukrainian Jews, numbering 214,000, were exterminated in the nefarious Belzec death camp, between Lvov and Lublin[14], in which 600,000 Jews, mostly from outside Ukraine, had perished.[15] Joshua Rubenstein[16] devotes considerable attention to moving "death vans" in which the Germans asphyxiated a total of 350,000 people in the occupied territories, including more than 100,000 Jews in Ukraine, by directing the engine exhaust into the sealed vehicles filled with the victims. Nevertheless, the

---

[13] Weiss, Aharon, *Encyclopedia of the Holocaust*, Vol. 3, pp. 572-575.
[14] Zabarko, Boris, op. cit., p. 389.
[15] Davies, Norman and Polonsky, Antony, cit., p. 274.
[16] Altman, Ilya and Rubenstein, Joshua, op. cit., p. 10.

overwhelming majority of the 1.6 million Jewish victims in Ukraine perished in open-air killings.

The operation to annihilate the Jews in the East began within a few weeks of the German army's occupation of a swath of Soviet territory. The diabolical methods the Germans used in the process included: relocation and concentration of the Jews to a minuscule fraction of the areas where they had lived; hermetically sealing the so-called ghettos; subjecting the incarcerated victims to hunger, illness, and torture; and then periodically hauling off portions of the ghetto to the town's outskirts, where they would often be forced to dig their own graves; and finally, machine-gunning and bulldozing them—dead or alive—into the pits.[17]

In Ukraine, specially trained executioners, organized in so-called *Einsatzgruppen* (C&D), conducted the mass killings, with the help of the S.S. *Wehrmacht* and Ukrainian gendarmes. The Ukrainian henchmen eagerly performed the grisly tasks of finding and getting the Jews out of their homes, guarding their march to the killing fields, forcing them to undress and line up for their executions, and pushing the victims into the mass graves.

According to *Yad Vashem* sources, the Holocaust essentially annihilated all Jews from 6,500 communities throughout Europe where Jews had comprised a significant or majority presence before the war. Assuming that Ukraine contained at least one-quarter of these communities and the annihilation of the Jews in each community required several hundred and, in some cases, thousands of Ukrainian gendarmes, one could conclude that several hundred-thousand Ukrainians had personally participated in the

---

[17] Zabarko, Boris, op. cit., p. xxiv.

heinous crime of exterminating their Jewish neighbors. The grisly events surrounding the killings of the Kiev Jews dramatically illustrates the essential role of the Ukrainians in these murders.

Within two weeks after their occupation of Kiev, the Germans, with the help of the Ukrainians, had managed in two days to assemble, haul to the infamous Babi Yar area, and execute more than 32,000 Jews. Such an enormous rate of killings, equivalent to 600 people per hour, must have required several thousand executioners, which the Germans could not spare at the height of their military operations, and must have involved, indeed, mostly Ukrainians. Many more Ukrainians most probably helped in rounding up the Jews and in seizing Jewish property.

Father Patrick Desbois has recently brought to light the horrors of these mass killings[18]. The author and his assembled organization have, during the last eight years, unearthed hundreds of the mass graves, documented eyewitness accounts of the mass killings, and, where possible, identified victims of the mass graves. In his March 2009 appearance in New York at the Museum of Jewish Heritage, the author stated that he had identified 700 Jewish mass graves in Ukraine and Belarus, and expressed his belief that he and his organization would identify a similar number of additional graves in the two countries.

It is significant to note that the Germans conducted the open-air mass killings in Ukraine near the towns where the Jews had lived and, most often in view of the local population, who, in fact, welcomed the Germans as their liberators from the Soviets. In this connection, about 25,000 young Ukrainians escaped from

---

[18] Desbois, Father Patrick, *The Holocaust By Bullets,* Palgrave Macmillan, 2008.

Western Ukraine to the German-occupied part of Poland after September 1939.[19] The Germans welcomed and trained most of these Ukrainians into death battalions, who participated in pogroms and murder of Jews.

A German contractor working on a military project for the German army recounts "bloodcurdling" scenes of the mass roundup and execution of the Jews in Rovno, Ukraine, on July 13, 1942. The mass action was conducted essentially by the Ukrainians, with the German commandant who issued the order simply standing by.

Expressing his own horror and revulsion, the contractor tells of the Ukrainian militiamen going from house to house, sadistically beating women, children and old men with the butts of rifles. They would gleefully find and rip a child from a mother's breast, and, holding the screaming infant by its legs, "they would ritualistically whirl the child several times overhead and smash it against a pillar."[20]

Since 1992, the Ukrainians, and particularly the Ukrainian government, have assiduously denied any involvement in the annihilation of Ukrainian Jews, while willfully covering sites of the mass graves with new construction, roads, or farmland. In fact, the widespread campaign of the Ukrainian government to wipe out the memory of the Holocaust in its historical records, as well as on the ground, has been fully documented.[21] Furthermore, turning the tables, Ukraine government blames the "Jewish Communists" for the ills that befell the Ukrainians after the war.

---

[19] Sabrin, B.F., op. cit., p. 8.

[20] Huneke, Douglas H., *The Moses of Rovno,* New York, Dodd, Mead & Co., 1985, p. 56.

[21] Bartov, Omer, *Erased,* New Jersey, Princeton University Press, 2007.

C. Conclusions and Reflections

The Jews in Ukraine lived in the same space and same historical timeframe as the Ukrainians, yet worlds apart from each other. Mostly urban, the Jews excelled, and often dominated, commerce, industry, finance, and the professions. The overwhelming majority of Ukrainians, by contrast, lived in the surrounding villages, tilling the soil and raising livestock; they had little education, and were easy targets of unscrupulous leaders. The economic and social divides became the source of violent uprisings and pogroms against the Jews through the centuries.

The Ukrainians' enmity against the Jews stemmed also from contrasting political objectives of the two peoples, particularly in the 20th century. The Ukrainians strove for independence from Russia, and since the Communist Revolution, from the Soviet Union. The Jews, on the other hand, were in the forefront of the Communist movement and revolution. These basic conflicts added to the primitive forces of envy, as well as to the old curse of anti-Semitism that had prevailed throughout Russia, formed an explosive mixture of Ukrainian anti-Semitic hatred to which the Germans gave free rein and direction.

The psychotic obsession of the Germans to kill every Jew made it difficult to rescue many. The exceptional courage and determination of the Danes, the Bulgarians, some villagers in France, and a significant number of "righteous gentiles" among the Ukrainians, supports the notion that the rescue of a substantial number of Jews was possible, particularly in the dense forests of the region. Tragically, hundreds of thousands of Ukrainians had chosen instead to actively participate in the extermination of the Jews. Sadly, the Ukrainian people—and the Ukrainian government—have been denying any responsibility for the demise of the

Jews in Ukraine and, instead, persist to blame their war losses on the Jews.

APPENDIX II

Death of the Jews in Dubno

A. Dubno, a Shtetl No More

Jews began to settle in Dubno, a town in Volhynia, Poland (today Ukraine), in the early 16th century, making it one of the oldest, and for four centuries, most important Jewish communities in Eastern Europe. At the beginning of the 17th century, Isaiah Ha-Levi Horowitz, author of Shenei Luchot Ha-Berit (Two Tablets of the Law), served as Dubno's Rabbi. The Jews numbered about 2,000 at the time of the Khmelnystski massacres of 1648-49, which murdered between 1,100 and 1,500 Jews who had sought, but were denied by the Poles, refuge in the local fortress.

Within a short time the community became the most important in the region and gained representation on the council of Volhynia. The owners of the town, Princes Lubormirski, accorded the Jewish community special privileges in 1699 and 1713, and by the beginning of the 18th century, Dubno had become the largest Jewish community in the district of Luck. The community gained representation on the Council of the Four Lands and earned the sobriquet "Dubno the Great" (Dubno Rabbati). In 1773, the Great Fair of Lvov moved to, and stayed for the following twenty years, in Dubno, which became an important commercial center, mainly in the trade of grain and hops.

One of the most famous of the 18th-century Jewish preachers of Lithuania, Yaacov Kranz, moved to Dubno and became an important leader of the community, earning the title the Maggid of Dubno. Economic prosperity of the Jews continued throughout the 18th century, leading the community of about 2,000 to build in 1782-1784 the Great Synagogue, an imposing structure perched on a hill, still in existence. The community maintained many cultural institutions, and there was an active Zionist and pioneer movement.

With the dismemberment of Poland towards the end of the century, Dubno came under Russian domination, and Jewish prosperity began to decline, although its population increased to 7,108 in 1897. Two fires, in 1878 and 1895, caused great damage and necessitated outside help to rehabilitate the community. During World War I and the Civil War in Russia (to 1921), the city changed hands a number of times, and the community suffered extreme hardship, as well as murderous riots by gangs of Simon Petlura, the leader of the short-lived Ukrainian state.

Between the two World Wars, Jews engaged in light industry and were prominent as exporters of hops and grains, with about 85 percent of petty trade of Dubno in Jewish hands. The community ran a hospital, orphanage, and old age home, while a Tarbut school reached an enrollment of 400, and a private Jewish high school another 120. All the Zionist parties were active, as well as many of the youth movements.

Shortly after the outbreak of World War II, Soviet forces had occupied Dubno, and dealt harshly with the Jewish community. Soviet authorities nationalized all enterprises and businesses, most of which were Jewish; they liquidated Jewish communal institutions, made all Jewish political parties illegal, arresting many of their leaders, among them David Perl, President of the

Zionist Organization; transferred Jewish welfare institutions to the municipality, allowing only one Jewish activity—the public kitchen for refugees from the west. On the eve of the German onslaught on the Soviet Union on June 22, 1941, the Jewish population of Dubno numbered approximately 12,000.

During the first few days of the war, several hundred young Jews fled Dubno to the interior of the Soviet Union. After the Germans entered Dubno (June 25), the local Ukrainian population indulged in acts of murder and robbery, while the Germans extracted 100,000 rubles from the Jewish community. On July 22, 1941, 80 Jews were executed by the Nazis in the local cemetery. On August 3, the Germans organized a Judenrat—a Jewish representation body—headed by Konrad Tojbenfeld. On August 21, 1941, 1,075 Jewish men were executed at the Jewish cemetery. The Jewish population was conscripted for forced labor, many succumbing to the unbearable conditions. The winter that followed (1941-42) was marked by hunger and disease, despite the attempts to provide relief by organizing public kitchens.

At the end of March 1942, the Germans invited the Ukrainians to "clean out" Jewish homes, while driving all the Jews into a ghetto and incarcerating them under a regime of starvation, terror, and forced labor. On May 27, the Nazi police moved in and "selected" over 5,000 "non-productive" Jews to be killed and buried in mass graves on the outskirts of the city. The destruction of the remnant of the community continued throughout the summer, and in October, in a final Action to liquidate the ghetto, the Germans, with the help of Ukrainians, murdered and buried in mass graves, 3,000 Jews, including about 150 discovered in hiding.

When the war was over, only about 400 Jews from Dubno remained alive, most of them survivors from the Soviet Union.

No Jewish community was reestablished after the war. A society of immigrants from Dubno has been established in Israel.

[Compiled from various sources of the Museum of the Jewish Diaspora in Tel Aviv, Israel]

B. Testimony of a Survivor of the Dubno Ghetto

Note: In 1995 the East Brunswick, N.J. Jewish Center held a service to commemorate the Holocaust, under the title "Dubno a Shtetl No More." Irene Tannen, a lawyer and a survivor of the Dubno ghetto, was invited to address the gathering. Following is a record of her remarks:

"We are assembled today for a memorial service for the parents and family members of Michael Kesler, Harold Greenspan, mine and all the thousand and thousands of Jews, who had been killed during the Nazi-Occupation time in our home town Dubno, Poland and all other places.

Michael Kesler and Harold Greenspan gave you a background about our home town and the events which followed immediately after the Germans crossed the Soviet border Sunday, June 22, 1941. Michael and Harold did not have to witness the human degradation, the life in the ghetto, the every day atrocities, the selection processes and finally the deaths of the beloved. I had witnessed all of these; I survived.

When Michael Kesler approached me to share the ghetto experiences, it was for me an emotional decision. During the more than fifty years which elapsed, I tried to suppress all these memories. After Michael's approach, I started to reconstruct the events. Here they are:

Sunday, June 22, 1941, and Monday, young men were being drafted, the Soviet administration—Police, City Hall and others

—were nervous waiting for directions from higher authorities. The high officials were putting their families on trains and trucks heading east. Jewish families were gathering to decide what to do —to stay or to escape; where to escape; how to escape; who of the family should escape. Big decisions; emotional decisions. The main concern of each family was the young people whom they considered to be most vulnerable. On June 24, 1941, we heard already some artillery activity, and on June 25th, the first SS Einsatzgruppen arrived in Dubno.

Two days later, the Einsatzgruppen swept the Jewish quarter and, with the assistance of the local Ukrainian paramilitary gangs, rounded up close to 800 Jewish males. They were marched to the Jewish cemetery, summarily executed, and their bodies thrown into huge dug-outs. Among these men was my older brother, who left behind his young wife and a three-year-old girl, Miriam; among those men was also the father of my girlfriend, with whom I survived, Rafael Bogdanow. The terror and the panic among the Jews were unbearable.

During the first week of invasion, the SS people began to organize the persecution and ultimate execution of the Jewish community. They established a Judenrat—a Jewish representation body—and they forced the Judenrat to submit names of the best-known and honorable Jews in town; these people were picked up and hanged in the town center. Then the German authorities issued an order for all Jews to wear an armband with the Star of David. This was followed by another order for Jews to deliver to the authorities all jewelry in their possession.

Then came the selection process of girls and young women. It began with the SS running through the Jewish homes and rounding up young women and girls into one crowded area. The SS people also searched in places around the house, where young women might be hiding. They herded the crowd and women on the street—whoever was there at the time—into a large restaurant. Following that, the SS searched for and apprehended women who had escaped and were hiding in surrounding areas; these women were also brought to the restaurant.

I was there. The SS were like wild animals. We were beaten with whips and forced into adjoining rooms. After many hours we were released; however, many of the victims disappeared, and were never heard from again.

While these atrocities were going on, the Jews had to work to get food. We sold whatever we could. Sometime in the middle of July, the German government forcibly transported the Jews from the surrounding small towns to Dubno, and placed them in designated areas along the whole length of Stara Street and its neighboring narrow side streets. This was the beginning of the Dubno Ghetto.

In the winter of 1941, we all were in the Ghetto. There was not enough food; the quarters were cold, and the older people and the children were getting ill and dying. The designated area for the Jews, the Ghetto, was small. During the winter of 1941, the Jews had to deliver furs to the German authorities. One of our school friends was arrested and shot because he was listening to news on the radio. It is hard for a human being to imagine the every day life in the Ghetto, the struggle to survive during the day and to see the beloved again in the evening. During that time, several actions took place, with several thousand people herded, marched out of the Ghetto, then shot and buried in the ravines at the outskirts of Dubno.

In the late summer of 1942, a large-scale action by the SS squads inflicted horrible deaths on nearly 3,000, in the Dubno Ghetto. I escaped during this action. The final liquidation of the

Dubno Ghetto was in October 1942. Several dozens of our brothers and sisters managed to escape the slaughter. They found refuge in the villages of mainly Czech and some Polish peasants who, in many cases, paid with their own lives and the lives of their families to save Jews. In my family, two children of my older sister found refuge, in the winter of 1943, in a small Czech village of about 30 families. The villagers decided that the children, ages seven and eight, would be every week in a different household. This lasted for over a year, and all the villagers, including the children, kept secret that the two Jewish children were hiding in their midst."

C. Testimony of a German Witness to the Dubno Executions

[A further step toward the carrying out of a policy of mass murder was the creation of the Einsatzgruppen. These special mobile killing units followed the German army into Eastern Europe where they rounded up Jews, often luring them by promising that they would be "resettled" elsewhere. At the trial of the Einsatzgruppen leaders at Nuremberg in 1947, Herman Graebe, manager of a German construction company, described how one group of victims was rounded up and executed in Dubno, Ukraine, on October 5, 1942.]

"My foreman and I went directly to the pits. I heard rifle shots in quick succession from behind one of the earth mounds. The people who had got off the trucks—men, women and children of all ages—had to undress upon the order of an S.S. man, who carried a riding or dog whip. They had to put down their clothes in fixed places, sorted according to shoes, top clothing and under-clothing. I saw a heap of shoes of about 800 to 1,000 pairs, great piles of underlinen and clothing.

"Without screaming or weeping, these people undressed, stood around in family groups, kissed each other, said farewells, and waited for a sign from another S.S. man who stood near the pit, also with a whip in his hand. During the 15 minutes that I stood near the pit, I heard no complaint or plea for mercy.

"An old woman with snow-white hair was holding a one-year-old child in her arms and singing to it and tickling it. The child was cooing with delight. The parents were looking on with tears in their eyes. The father was holding the hand of a boy about 10 years old and speaking to him softly; the boy was fighting his tears. The father pointed to the sky, stroked his head and seemed to explain something to him.

"At that moment, the S.S. man at the pit shouted something to his comrade. The latter counted off about 20 persons and instructed them to go behind the earth mound. I remember well a girl, slim and with black hair, who as she passed close to me, pointed to herself and said: 'twenty-three years old.'

"I walked around the mound and found myself confronted by a tremendous grave. People were closely wedged together and lying on top of each other so that only their heads were visible. Nearly all had blood running over their shoulders from their heads. Some of the people were still moving. Some were lifting their arms and turning their heads to show that they were still alive. The pit was already two-thirds full. I estimated that it contained about a thousand people. I looked for the man who did the shooting. He was an S.S. man, who sat at the edge of the narrow end of the pit, his feet dangling into the pit. He had a Tommy-Gun on his knees and was smoking a cigarette.

"The people, completely naked, went down some steps and clambered over the heads of the people lying there to the place to which the S.S. man directed them. They lay down in front of the dead or wounded people; some caressed those who were still alive and spoke to them in a low voice. Then I heard a series of shots. I looked into the pit and saw that the bodies were twitching or the heads lying already motionless on top of the bodies that lay beneath them. Blood was running from their necks.

"The next batch was approaching already. They went down into the pit, lined themselves up against the previous victims and were shot."

(Reference: Huneke, Douglas K., op. cit., p. 189.)

APPENDIX III

Barbarossa

T he following is a sketchy account of a heavy, complex war. It is intended to provide a guide—albeit a superficial one—to the events and travels described in the main chapters.

The material in this Appendix, and the figures given in the table below, are taken from the references quoted at the end of the Appendix. Note that the references are relatively recent, post-war studies.

Overview

Barbarossa, the code name for Hitler's onslaught on the Soviet Union, the most massive military operation in history up to that time, began on June 22, 1941. At its initial stage, the operation involved the following, estimated forces:

	Germany and Allies	Red Army
Divisions	166	190
Personnel	4,306,800	3,289,851
Guns and mortars	42,601	59,787
Tanks (incl. assault guns)	4,171	15,687
Aircraft	4,846	10,743

Source: Mikhail Meltyukhov, Stalin's Missed Chance, *Table 47, p. 445*

Initial Phase

At the beginning of the war, the front stretched for approximately 1,500 kilometers, from the Black to the Baltic Seas. The German onslaught was organized in three theaters; Leningrad in the north; Belarus, Smolensk, and Moscow in the center; and Lvov and Kiev in the South. The ultimate destination of the central theater was Moscow. The southern theatre aimed its assault at capturing Ukraine and Stalingrad, the gateway to Azerbaijan oil, and it encompassed the axis of Rovno, Lutsk, and Dubno, my hometown.

The First Week of Disaster

During the first week of Barbarossa, the Soviets suffered enormous losses of thousands of aircraft on the ground, thousands of tanks, and over a million soldiers. They also lost essentially all the territories they had acquired from 1939 until 1941. A number of factors contributed to these heavy losses:

- Surprise of the onslaught: In the early hours of June 22, the Germans managed, by surprise, to bomb the Soviets' airfields and practically eliminate its combat Air Force. Elements of surprise also helped the Germans clear large areas of the Soviets' defense lines.
- Lack of Soviets' preparedness: The Soviets had enormous amounts of equipment, and infantry men to defend the border, but no unified organization to coordinate and effectively utilize these forces. They lacked communications and efficient organization. The shadow of Stalin and fear of retribution paralyzed the initiative of individual commanders. The failures of the Soviets to decisively defeat the

small Finnish army a year earlier had spread a heavy pall of apprehension and timidity in the armed forces.

- Poor roads: John Erickson in his book, *On the Run to Stalingrad*, vividly describes Soviet tanks being lined up, as sitting ducks, on impassible roads in Belarus and Ukraine, making it easy for the German Luftwaffe to destroy them en masse.
- Superiority of German forces: The Soviets may have had more tanks and more aircraft than the Germans, but most of them were of a much older vintage. The Soviet Air Force, whatever survived the massive elimination of Soviet aircraft on the ground, proved no match to the new *Messerschmitts*. And the superbly trained German soldiers fought with a ferocity and skillfulness unknown to Soviet soldiers.
- A wavering allegiance of Soviet population: The Ukrainians and the Byelorussians, particularly in the areas conquered by the Soviets in 1939, were hostile to the Soviet regime. Many Ukrainian soldiers surrendered (only to be later killed by the Germans).

Despite the disadvantages and the setbacks, Soviet commanders—individually or in unison with others—mounted significant counterattacks, which slowed the German advance, particularly east of the old Polish-Russian border.

Lutsk–Rovno–Dubno Axis of Combat

This axis became the center of intensive fighting in the first week of Barbarossa. The single most critical event took place on June 25, 1941, at Brody, 60 kilometers southwest of Dubno, with a clash between large tank forces of the two armies. The German panzer divisions outnumbered and outmaneuvered the Soviets, and won a decisive battle that opened the eastward gates of the axis.

A major reason for Soviet defeat at Brody was the Soviets' inability to supply more tanks to the ensuing battle, mainly due to poor roads and poor communications. Meanwhile, German Panzer Division 11 penetrated northeast of Brody and on June 25 arrived in Dubno (approximately 12 hours after my sister and I had left home). Soviet forces, Mechanized Divisions 228, 213 and Tank Division 43 counter attacked and pushed the Germans back. However, two days later, on June 27th, the Germans retook Dubno. Later that day, they entered Ostrog about the same time my sister and I were leaving Ostrog. Two days later, German forces crossed the old Soviet-Polish border and entered Shepetovka, where we had caught the last train east a few hours earlier.

At the same time, big clashes took place between the Soviet and German forces around Lvov, approximately 150 kilometers southwest of Dubno. On June 29, General Vlasov, a Ukrainian, commanding a major motorized Soviet army, surrendered. Thus, within one week of Barbarossa, the Germans reached the old Soviet-Polish border of Ukraine, and opened the roads for their advance towards Kiev, the capital of Ukraine. At the same time, Romanian forces, allied with Germany, penetrated deeply along the Black Sea towards Odessa.

References

Erickson, John. *The Road to Stalingrad, Stalin's War with Germany: Volume 1*. New Haven: Yale University Press, 1975.

Glantz, David. *The Initial Period of War on the Eastern Front*: Proceedings of the Fourth Art of War Symposium. London: Frank Cass & Co, 1993.

Zhukov, Georgy. *The Memoirs of Marshall Zhukov*, University of Oklahoma Press, 1971.

APPENDIX IV

Selected Maps

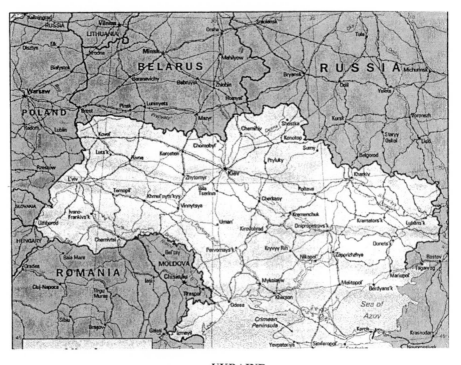

UKRAINE
(From www.lib.utexas.edu/maps/commonwealth/ukraine.gif)

**SOUTHEAST RUSSIA, KAZAKHSTAN,
AND A PORTION OF CENTRAL ASIA**
(From www.lib.utexas.edu/maps/commonwealth/Kazakhstan.jpg)

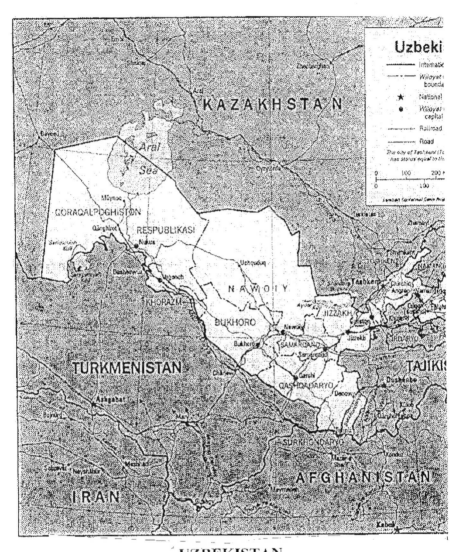

UZBEKISTAN
(From www.lib.utexas.edu/maps/commonwealth/uzbekistan.jpg)

APPENDIX V

Chapter 10 Poem Set to Music (p. 161)

Homecoming to Dubno the Ukraine in 1945

Based on an adopted theme from Tchaikovsky's Violin Concerto

Michael Kesler
after Pyotr Ilyich Tchaikovsky

Acknowledgements

This memoir had a long gestation period. The horrors of my World War II experiences would sometimes haunt me at night or, triggered by an unpleasant occurrence, parade before me as if they had happened the day before. I had kept memories of those experiences hidden within me for over sixty years and have longed for years to set them free to tear apart their lock on me. My opportunity to do so came a few years ago, when I joined an adult education class in Princeton, New Jersey in creative writing, led by a professional writer, Hanna Fox. Slowly, methodically, the idea of writing about the six most memorable years of my life began to take shape.

I wish to express my thanks to Hanna Fox for introducing me to, and shepherding me through, the exciting world of writing and publishing. I am grateful to Rhoda Blecker, a published writer, for editing the manuscript and a subsequent revision of it, and to Dr. Walter Brasch, Professor of Journalism at Bloomsburg University in Pennsylvania, for in-depth editing of the final and an earlier version of the manuscript, as well as for valuable advice on publishing the book. I sincerely appreciate the moving, personal Foreword Dr. Manus Midlarsky, Professor of Political Science at Rutgers University has written.

I am profoundly grateful to my wife, Dr. Barbara S. Reed,

Associate Professor of Journalism and Media Studies at Rutgers University for the endless late-night and early-morning hours she has devoted to prepare the manuscript on its way to the printers. I feel much obliged to my colleagues, friends, and relatives who have read, commented, and helped propel the manuscript for publication. And, I want to express my sincere thanks to Laura Cier, my secretary, who has patiently typed, read, and re-typed the hundreds of pages that have gone into the making of this book, even while I have been losing my eyesight. Last but not least, I am most thankful to the staff members of Strategic Book Group, the publisher, who have guided me smoothly and beautifully through the process of turning my manuscript into a finished, commercial product.

Michael G. Kesler
July 2, 2010
East Brunswick, New Jersey

About the Book

On June 24, 1941, Michael, 16, and his sister Luba, 19, leave their home in Dubno in Ukraine, just ahead of the advancing German armies. Fleeing by foot and by train deep into Ukraine and beyond, the siblings spend a brutal winter in a town near Stalingrad, where they nearly perish from hunger and cold. In July 1942, they escape again ahead of the Germans' onslaught on Stalingrad. A young thief thwarts their attempt to leave Stalingrad by ship, as he snatches the golden watch that their Father had given to Michael. In the commotion, Michael loses his queue to board the ship which, however, tragically hits a mine and sinks.

Leaving Stalingrad two weeks later, the siblings travel to Uzbekistan, where Michael works as a veterinary assistant and Luba as a teacher. In the fall of 1943, both fall ill with typhoid and Luba nearly dies. In early spring 1944, Michael joins the Soviet army and encounters violence from a hostile soldier, who threatens to kill him. Having lost all contact, Luba desperately begins a long search for Michael. Finding him, finally, in the military camp, she orchestrates his escape. The siblings leave for Samarkand, where Michael becomes a weaver, and Luba the seller of the cloth.

In the fall of 1945, Michael, and Luba, joined by a friend—soon to become her husband—return to Dubno and witness the mass graves of the town's nearly all 8,000 Jews. They travel to Krakow, joining the surviving mother and several cousins of Luba's husband, who had been saved working in Schindler's factories. They leave for the U.S. Occupation Zone of West Germany and enter the Landsberg displaced persons' camp.

About the Author

ichael G. Kesler, Ph.D., a chemical engineering graduate of MIT and New York University, worked and consulted for the petroleum industry. After retiring in 2006, he engaged in writing this memoir of his experiences during World War II. He has also edited and published his late wife's book, "Grit—A Pediatrician's Odyssey From a Soviet Camp to Harvard," (AuthorHouse). In addition to professional publications, he has, over the years, published a number of poems and short stories. His name has appeared in "Who's Who in the East" and in "American Men of Science."

He and his wife, Dr. Barbara S. Reed, associate professor of Journalism and Media Studies at Rutgers University, have six children and 11 grandchildren, and reside in East Brunswick, New Jersey.

Breinigsville, PA USA
04 November 2010
248666BV00002B/4/P